Watching
the fire-eater

Robert Minhinnick
Watching
the fire-eater

Seren is the book imprint of Poetry Wales Press Ltd
57 Nolton Street, Bridgend, Wales, CF31 3AE
01656 663018
www.serenbooks.com

ISBN 1-85411-075-6

A CIP record for this title is available from the British Library

The publisher acknowledges the financial
assistance of the Welsh Books Council

Printed in Palatino by Berforts Information Press Limited

Cover photographs: Eamon Bourke

Contents

Acknowledgements

Thanks are due to John Barnie and Jo Menell for their encouragement and assistance. I am especially grateful to the Welsh Writers' Trust for the John Morgan Award in 1989-90.

Some of these essays previously appeared in *Planet* and *Poetry Wales*.

Introduction

Recently in Prague I observed a curious incident. I was standing with a small crowd at the shrine in Wenceslas Square dedicated to Jan Palach, who burned himself to death in protest at the Soviet invasion of Czechoslovakia in 1968. A woman with a bunch of flowers stepped into the shrine area itself. She attempted to lay her bouquet with the numerous other floral tributes and scraps of writing that had been left within the small garden.

Immediately another woman, rotund, almost elderly, detached herself from the crowd and began to abuse the tribute-bringer. The first woman looked baffled, then startled, as the tirade continued. She attempted to shrug off the interruption and advanced further into the garden. The second woman pursued her and began to scream. She then attempted to beat the flowers from the other's hands. Failing in this, she started to rain blows on the back and shoulders of the second woman, who now obviously considering discretion her wisest choice, retreated to the square after quickly scattering her blooms.

Still shouting, but now rhetorically, and for the benefit of our small crowd, the attacker stood within the shrine and carefully picked up each of these flowers. With operatic disdain she bent the stems and shook off the petals, before flinging them away. Slowly we dispersed, leaving her muttering and triumphant.

Putting together this collection of essays, I feel a little like the woman who ventured out of the square and into the garden. The keepers of such places are notoriously hard to please. Carry the wrong flowers, or have the nerve to trespass, and their reaction might be severe.

Poets are often seduced by the melancholic pleasures of cultural alienation. This fastidiousness means their work is easy to dismiss as a cry from the sidelines of life. This might apply to my poetry, or in this case, my prose. Yet here they are, eighteen pieces from the last seven years, my nervous progress through the shrines. And if there are redundancies here, or talent to be startled by the searingly obvious, so be it. Matters of 'the environment' loom large, but for many we already live in an age of post-environmental concern that a brief period ago might have appeared a product of science fiction. America too is present, that endless source of vicarious engagements with the dangerous and absurd. But the bulk of the collection is taken up with Wales, a country increasingly difficult to locate as it sloughs an identity of clichés.

Time is not always kind to the essay. Or not to the type I seem to write. And if it is true that those writers who look for consolation in their own work are the ones most prepared to believe in lies, at least I now know where to begin the rest of the journey.

Robert Minhinnick, May 1992

Rio de Journal

1

It's oddly comforting to note that Rio de Janeiro, city of marvels, has a branch of C & A's. Two floors of dull clothes, not particularly cheap. No-one in Copacabana but me, it seems, is wearing any of them. In fact, no-one but me is wearing any clothes in Copacabana today.

It's 10 a.m. and 38°C. I'm reluctant to take off my shirt because my tanning has so far been done in segments. Like some Gwent rugby team I am decked out in red and white hoops. Red knees, white shins, black Clarks shoes, with exhausted, wafer-like heels.

Everyone else has bare feet. The men pose where the surf breaks, muscles oiled like the grain of some dark tropical hardwood. The women meanwhile have all been to the dentist's. Their bodies sport the Rio bikini known as 'dental floss'. An alarming garment, this, for someone brought up on the rolled up jeans and cover-everything-just-in-case swimsuits of Trecco Bay.

All that the Copacabana woman wears is a brilliant G-string and a pair of sunglasses. I look at the islands in the bay, fringed with tropical forest. I turn to the granite pinnacle of Corcovado, with its immense concrete Christ, arms greeting all-comers to the city. False icon. Rio welcomes no-one who cannot pay his way. And half Brazil's population, malnourished and illiterate, are too busy counting huge bankrolls of almost worthless old cruzerio notes to look that far into the sky.

You reach the summit of Corcovado on the 'cog train', a slow ascent through Tijuca, the city's own remnant of Atlantic forest. Hummingbirds gleam in the flowers and plastics around the track; electric blue butterflies, wings bigger than banknotes, float over the train on its way to an astounding view. But from here the statue seems as incongruous as King Kong waving from the

Empire State.

I lie on the crystalline sand, its creamy demerara sprinkled with a million ring-pulls and the brown, lipsticked butts of Hollywoods. Vigilant against the heat which I can actually feel doing me harm, I am also irradiated by paranoia. Brazil is the second most violent country in the world. (Colombia, to the north, tops the league.) Rio is the capital of that violence. And the beach at Copacabana is the most likely place in the capital to get rolled. There's no way of disguising my foreigner status as I spreadeagle on bathmat and struggle with a broken-spined Margaret Atwood. I've met plenty of pale Brazilians but my pallor is different. It has the greeny look of the underside of a strawberry. There is something shameful about it. Or obscene. In the streets like everybody else I wear dirty tee-shirts and darned shorts. And still the posses of moneychangers, the street committees of orphans with offers of stolen sweets and postcards, home unerringly in on my tropical virginity.

But there are no obvious mobsters here. My neighbours are enormous rosewood-coloured grandmothers, hawkers with trays of coconut, a bodybuilder with face mutilated by the black slash of sunglasses. And a one-legged boy who has planted his crutch like a palmtree in the sand, as if defying the waves to fell it. Bring no money to the beach is the dictum. Or only enough to appease. The sun lays an anvil on my back, the surf shouts and murmurs deliriously like a hospital ward at night. And when I rise, my body shines in a white chrysalis of sand. Opening my eyes is to emerge from a fever, the druggy traumas and insane dreams of meningitis I remember as a child. A doctor came and asked me to touch my throat with my chin. I couldn't. She pierced my spine with an enormous hypodermic and made me count to thirty-five. Thirty-five tigers, thirty-five bowls of fruit. She taught me to walk when I fell across the bed, my colt's legs stiff, unrooted, my face pressed into the sand-white apron of her lap.

My bag is gone, my poor-man's plastic bag with watch and books and oil. But my shape is there, sculpted in the sand. The rebirth is over and I can see again, I can talk to the beautiful, concerned families under their parasols, and they shake their heads, offer money, warnings.

Twenty yards away I find a neat stack of lotion bottle and

paperbacks. The watch, which is cheap, but belongs to my daughter, is missing. Now I can walk, almost steadily to the surf, and clean away the hard carapace of crystals on my back and feel no fear. Eat the rich, says the lyric in my head. Eat the rich and set them free, and I tiptoe into the democracy of the waves, with the rosewood grandmothers, the sleek cripple who knifes through a sea that is really quite ludicrously blue. I look at his crutch, still firm in the sand, and all around it now lie the flowers of the surf.

Coming out of C & A's I saw a dead man on the pavement. Naked but for a pair of filthy shorts, he lay scrunched up like a ball of paper. His face pressed in the dust, lips fixing the cement with a dry kiss. At least he looked as if he should be dead. If so, this was my second corpse. There was one at a bus stop two weeks previously on the main road between Rio and Resende. A man sprawled stiffly, ridiculously in the hammering sun. No-one stopped, and the traffic poured on.

Perhaps that other was not dead, perhaps the busy shopfront on Avenida Nossa Senhora de Copacabana was his home. People sleep in boxes here, in cardboard corrals on the pavements, on the burnt grass of traffic islands, on the oil stains between parked cars, in the marble porches of banks. Whatever, no-one remarked, no-one paid the body the slightest heed. I stepped over his legs and made for the bus stop.

Now we race across Rio on a bucking 127, clinging to the rail after paying 20 new cruzados – equivalent to 20,000 old cruzados – in notes as dirty and wrinkled as the old British ten bobs I can still remember. Here you enter the body of the bus through a turnstile. That is, if you are lucky and avoid the rush hour. Yesterday, coming back from the Botanical Gardens, still thinking of the dragonflies and white herons, the smooth bark, silky as an erect penis, of the avenue of palms, we had our first confrontation with the thieves who work the bus routes.

A girl with the hair of Monroe and eyes of a barracuda blocked us in the usual mêlée at the turnstile, whilst other gang members attempted to go through our pockets. I felt their hands breeze over my body, their practised tugs at the zips of the haversack. For what seemed an age I was too surprised to move, and then surprised myself by pushing the blonde hard between the breasts and escaping over the turnstile's clicking wheel.

11

'They got nothing,' I boasted, squashed into the safety of a seat, along with the secretaries and schoolgirls. 'The bastards.'

There's nothing like a Rio bus ride. All of the traffic here is fast and impatient, but there's no-one more road cynical, not even a Rio taxi-driver, than a Rio bus-driver cleaving, in uniform of dark glasses, stubble and stick of gum, between the yellow shoals of cabs, leaving the Volkswagens shuddering in his wake. The buses are clean, cheap, and what's better, frequent. They make the city work. If you catch the wrong one it's usually no disaster, as long as you get off before being deposited in some scorching slum, or *favela*, which like enormous houses of cards, have grown up in the hills around the city.

Getting off in the Centro, or business district, we keep an appointment at the *Berlin*. This is a German restaurant with such savage air conditioning that it must be powered by its own nuclear reactor. The word is that it is owned by Nazis, and momentarily it seems possible that the Maitre D is himself an ancient blackshirt, his decayed flunkey's regalia greening with age, and no less impressive for that.

M has a succession of different sucos, orange, papaya, and something Amazonian, all divine fruit juices, almost unbearably cold. They must drink these in Valhalla or wherever expired Nazis go. I have chopp, a straw-coloured pilsner sparkling with foam. The glass is a tube of frost.

Avocado, salad, sucos, chopp. Our guest is Ivo Dawney, Brazilian correspondent for the *Financial Times*, and possessor of an office with perhaps the best view I have ever seen. Rio's harbour, its shipping, the bay with its forested islands, and an immense sky, are framed in his window behind a no less impressive savanna of desk, immaculate with single penholder and telephone.

It is Ivo who bargains with the Nazis, who orders the food, who recommends the drinks. It is Ivo who takes a napkin and draws routemaps for us through the rainforest and mountains, the slums and red-light districts of Rio State. It is Ivo who eats meat while we indulge in a chaste, macrobiotic interlude from the spluttering grills and eye-watering *cafezinhos* – those thimblefuls of diesel – of Rio's luncheon stands. And it is Ivo who must depart to his eyrie between the obsidian plinths of banks and the pinnacles of petroleum companies, whilst we are

12

still watching our breath cloud over the sucos, the winking eyes of the blond beer.

When the bill arrives on a silver plate held by a liverish Gestapo officer, I find it is thousands and thousands of cruzados more than all the cruzados I have folded in my money-belt, now cutting a permanent tribute to paranoia into my abdomen. Five times I count what I have and each time it seems to get smaller. We are the only customers now, and the black-uniformed waiters loll against the far wall, like a firing-squad ready to go on duty. The subdued music ceased long ago. Whatever you do, goes the advice, don't get involved with the police. Do anything this side of legal that stops you getting too close. I abandon M, frost-bitten over her goblet, and pursue the glamorous Ivo to his skyscraper, where he is composing a piece on the revolutionary financial plans of the new president, Ferdinand Collor, whilst making a trans-atlantic call to his mother. He lends me fifteen quid without interrupting either, and after half an hour I am back behind the studded doors of *Berlin*, where M has shrunk, like the ice in her glass, to a state of transparent, unrecognisable meekness. There are just enough cruzados left to hustle our way on to a 119 back towards Copacabana and our hotel deposit safe.

2

There is one bus per day to Maringa. We wait for an hour and join the mêlée at the door when it arrives. There are forty seats, but somehow eighty people have managed to squeeze themselves in.

Soon the paved road is left behind and we are driving up a track of orange dirt. The route is a series of steep hairpins that takes us further towards Anghulas Negras, the highest peak in Rio de Janeiro State and one of Brazil's tallest mountains.

The forest becomes thicker, an immense green blanket over the slopes, punctuated occasionally by trees of yellow and purple flowers. We stop once at a jungle station to pour water into the steaming radiator. Everyone piles off to buy beer or coke and use the toilet cubicles, made entirely and ingeniously from drinks cans.

Getting off the bus we walk up a hill to the wall of the forest. It is padlocked against us. Shut tight. M puts her hand against the first tree and pierces herself with its thorns. They leave a constellation of blood upon the palm. Foliage sprouts with spines, stems bristle like hairbrushes. There is a path that twists away from us which we decide not to take. Emerging in the clearing where our empty bus is waiting, we shake dust and heavy seeds from our clothes. It is starting to rain, and half naked, gleaming with the downpour, young men are wrestling round the huts.

The road is steeper, the bus slower, but there are still seventy people, clinging to every rail. It's pitch black when we drive into a paved square surrounded by a few dimly-lit houses. Turning off the engine, we encounter the sound of the forest, the insect whine as monotonous as a chainsaw.

There's lightning now, in silver veins over the mountains, and approaching thunder. Everybody disappears immediately into the darkness and we are left with our rucksacks and the very slightest feeling of panic. M is succinct about our position: 'Where the fuck are we?'

As chief navigator I should know, but inwardly I am cursing all those seductive books with titles like *A Brazilian Travel Survival Kit* and *South America on a Shoestring*. Actually I have already begun to doubt the showy 'integrity' of their approach to travelling in the Third World. Aimed at people who 'know how to get their luggage off the airport carousel', they feign to despise conventional Western tourists and tourist behaviour. The books definitely help to get you into places you would never otherwise have dreamed of, but their constant advice to 'budget travellers' on how to wring as much local colour and 'peak experiences' from a country, while putting in as little money as possible, is starting to pall. Whose bloody shoestring is it anyway?

The locals don't want our good intentions. They don't care about our curiosity, or our insatiable appetites for the unusual. They want our cash. That is something simple I can understand. Moreover, it's the only thing we've really got to offer. The lightning now looks like the reflection of some phenomenal explosion that has occurred behind the mountains. We walk into the dark.

3

Clarice Lispector is described as Latin America's greatest woman writer. Her stories are weird and brilliant, compulsive fragments that blend the disturbing with the absurd.

I read her carefully, lingering over each page. I don't want this book to end. The days are slow here, they allow you such indulgence, while the weather continues humid and treacherous. The hammock rocks gently, the hummingbird drinks from the rain-filled hibiscus a yard from my hand. Its bill is a hypodermic it inserts into every flower on the bush. In the distance, Anghulas Negras pushes a broken tusk through the rainforest. All the afternoon, Lispector's heroines, middle-class, Europeanized Brazilian women, writhe in their anguish, the intolerability of time.

In the morning we had ventured north into the forest. The rain dripped off the bamboo leaves, down the green organpipes of the bamboo trunks. We could hear the waterfall for half an hour before we saw it, a not quite distinguishable conversation in another room. A yellow magpie cruised between the wooded slopes of the valleys, the butterflies eluded by microseconds our succession of lenses. The trail wound through the mountains and into another state, famous for gold and thunder.

It did not matter that travellers had been here before us, horsemen, farmers, the owners of the Swiss-style wooden chalets that were now being built in the hills, each with their garland of semi-wild garden. Here the forest was accessible but not tamed. The sap whined in the trees like a television set left on after closedown, the mosquitos hung their barbed wire under the leaves.

And then there was the waterfall. Modest enough by Brazilian standards, this eighty foot high cataract immediately fulfilled any need I possessed for a glimpse of the natural world's ferocity. The river simply slid across a great cranium-round rock, and into space. It hung there like a staircase of water, a glass elevator outside an office block.

We stretched out on the flat boulders at the lip of the fall and peered into the haze of spray. Now the water voices had turned from conspiracy to revolution, yet we had found a position of intense calm. Butterflies drank from sockets in the stone, we explored the banks and caverns until slowly the sun crushed us into immobility. We lay under its javelins on the broad sandstone skull and studied the geometry of water that passed from the horizontal to the vertical, before the detonation in the prismatic cauldron below.

It is too hot here for meals in the day, especially as breakfast is usually a gargantuan feast of starch. But the clouds are massing grey and purple over the summits, and the first strange pinpoints of light are beginning to appear. Of the familiar constellations I can recognise only Orion and Gemini. But these are back to front, like a book with its cover printed the wrong way. What's cheering is that the Milky Way is extraordinarily rich, a twisted hammock of stars across the night.

Time to eat. There's nowhere to go but the front room of the family we are staying with. Beautiful, generous country people, they are completely baffled by our presence here. Or should I say our total lack of Portuguese. Arriving without a word of the language was a mixture of bravado, laziness and our inbred sense of cultural superiority. So it is gestures, smiles and inward groans as the platter of white rice appears yet again, the familiar cauldron of purple beans, the tough manioc. But there's also salad, meat, bread, wine, beer and orange juice. If Brazilians can't cook, they at least don't stint on the portions.

This afternoon our hosts startled us by bringing to our door, like a doctor or psychiatrist, an exiled American who has moved into a remote farmstead in the hills. The mother, father and fifteen-year-old daughter in baseball cap and English tee shirt thought we might be hungry or ill. Or lost. Or mad. Or all of these together. So they smilingly pushed the interpreter towards us, who translated their wonder at our arrival at their home. Actually, it seemed, they were very proud that we were staying with them, even if conversation was limited to issues of time, meals, and always introduced by my favourite Brazilian word, the greeting *Oi!* to which I was able to give endless subtle and meaningful nuances.

Languages are my downfall. Speaking a foreign language, I seem to lose my identity. Some people tell me it is a great freedom, a hugely liberating experience, to cast off the weight of their first, tyrannically domineering tongue. But for me, living without

English is like having a power cut in the house. My lifestyle is dependent on the electricity supply. If I reach for the socket or the switch and discover it isn't there, immediate panic takes over.

Welsh isn't a foreign language to me. I have been learning it all my life, but am still reluctant to speak it anywhere. In a pub in Beddgelert I remember once speaking in Welsh all night to a group of fence erectors and unemployed local youths. They remorselessly refused any recourse to English, even when I was floundering in puzzlement and incomprehension at the depths of their Gwynedd accents. I was another person, I became someone completely different, a stranger to myself, a bit of a buffoon in the bar, a terrifyingly helpless and uncertain *me*. But I kept English out, I kept it at bay. It was like refusing to open the door when someone you love has called round. A small, pathetic triumph for a linguistic remedial.

Now, hearing English again, whilst an enormous bug pursued a manic orbit around our porch light, was surprisingly comforting. But we could not explain ourselves. There was no particular reason why we should be where we were. We had simply arrived. In three days more, I said, we would be gone. To somewhere else where we will simply arrive. It was difficult to know if the family understood this, but tonight we have a marvellous meal with them, and they laugh and joke with us, and we drink their wine and there are toasts all round.

The father, black hair, curly, going grey, is proud of his wine. We see him every morning go off on his motorbike, and return at dusk, speckled with the orange mud of the roads. His wife and daughter stay home, cooking, laundering, tending their hillside gardens. English is taught at many of the schools in Brazil, but then so is French and German in British comprehensives. The daughter's English comprises about three words, one of which is *hello*. She is a beautiful girl, tremendously shy. But her baseball cap is worn at an international angle. She is the one who brings our food to the table, who takes away our dinner plates. When we give her some money, she is innocently amazed. Her parents come in and look at her proudly. She stares at the notes as if they were a letter written in a foreign language.

I want to hug the whole family, but instead pour another glass of the thin red. There is a guilt here, a disappointment. Because I know that this is as close as we are going to get to the ordinary people of Brazil. This humid evening high amongst the trees, with the racket of frogs and crickets outside, and the peculiar stars above the black horizon of peaks, this is as close as we are ever going to get to anything here. To anything on a personal level. And this is the place where gradually, I can relax and slowly drop my defences. To sit more comfortably back in my chair. Then the lightning jumps over the mountains and we watch its crazy athletics from the window. Predictably, the electricity fails. Our dining room is full of sudden darkness and knowing laughter. And still this is the place that almost feels like home.

4

The parachutes fall into the swamps and turn into herons. The palms are shaped exactly like immense green Coca Cola bottles. Tins rust where the mangroves once thrived. Our bus plunges on down the coast road, and I read again in the guide book how best to plan a visit to Brazil.

Apparently it is unwise to have a blood transfusion here. This seems like prejudice. I cannot imagine an introduction to Paris or San Francisco giving similar instructions. But, the text continues, if you are determined to travel, ensure you and your companion share the same blood group. I look at M. We don't match. Different letters of the alphabet circulate in our veins. So we make a pact not to bleed too much. We already know that back in Wales our blood when offered at donor sessions will only be used for plasma. The red corpuscles, because of the infinitesimal chances of containing sleeping-sickness picked up over here, will be useless. It's an odd feeling of rejection, combined with shallow pride. We are tainted at last by the exotic. We carry the mark of the tropics in our hearts.

There is a stop at Furnes to pick up workers at the power station. This is Brazil's only nuclear plant, and possesses an appalling record of low productivity and high costs. Good to know, says M, that nuclear power behaves in the same way here as it does at home. Wedged into a bay below the high walls of Atlantic forests, Furnes looks jerry-built and temporary, its great dome, seen from the road, resembling a grubby skull-cap. The plant has its own neat village, with laundry, shops and cinema, a little world with a special secret. Its irradiated water, of course, flows into the sea, and around the coastline of forested islands that we will explore tomorrow. Further out in the bay, it is claimed, lie some of the world's greatest oil reserves.

The dusk is stiflingly warm. You wear it like a coat. Under each of the few streetlights hangs a blizzard of flies, while down at the harbour the lizards cling to whitewashed houses and the sewers flow slowly into the sea's lagoon. The nearest beach is a blue, shining field of excrement. Above it the vultures gloat in the palms, maintaining a surly picket in the fronds.

The skipper adjusts the position of the boat by a short burst of the engine. I watch the petrol waste spread behind us in a rainbow, smell the brief combustion. Even in Rio's most congested streets, what we discovered is a relative absence of traffic pollution. In London, Cardiff, even in corners of rural Powys at the height of the tourist season, the concentration of low level ozone in the atmosphere, created by the action of sunlight on exhaust gases, can be high above the World Health Organisation warning limits. In Athens, some three hundred people are admitted daily to hospital suffering the ill-effects of traffic pollution. These feelings of headache, eye irritation, sore throat, the universal city rush-hour flu, are caused largely by poisonous ozone. In Japan, Mexico, USA, it has killed people.

Perhaps the same goes for Brazil, but here many of the cars run on 'alcool', a fuel derived from sugar-cane. It might be my imagination, but the city air does taste sweeter, despite the ever-present flotillas of diesel-guzzling buses. For once it might be that economic and environmental priorities are agreed to be the same. With the use of alcool, Brazil's petroleum imports are cut, and the country uses instead a common, easily-grown crop. Ah yes, but do they flatten rainforest to grow it, asks the green spy in my head.

That Brazil is bent on destroying its tree cover is a global commonplace. It is now removing 50,000 square kilometres of forest every year, largely to turn thin and easily exhausted and eroded rainforest soils into temporary farmlands. Worldwide, such devastation now continues at the rate of two acres every second, and the burning rainforests contribute one tenth of all the gases responsible for the greenhouse effect.

The bright chiffon of petrol has now spread round the rocks behind us. Of course, the burning of alcool adds to global warming, pumping invisible and odourless carbon dioxide into the atmosphere. Even our blameless, miraculous lungs exhale the poison. Each year we send four billion tonnes of the stuff into the sky, helping to imprison the sun's reflected heat. The burning of Amazonia creates more than two thirds of the total carbon dioxide generated each year by the UK.

We get out of the boat and pay the owner. The last five hours have been spent on a series of islands where the mountains plunge into the bay and the trees seem to go on forever. It is hard to believe that Brazil has destroyed all but 5 per cent of its Atlantic forest cover, with in fact, only 2 per cent of primary forests remaining here.

Tree planting is vital to combat the crisis. It has been estimated that we need to replant 4 million square kilometres in tropical areas to help absorb that 4 billion tonnes of carbon dioxide the world adds annually to the atmosphere. It is claimed this would cost about 160 billion dollars, and, running parallel to massive commitments to energy efficiency and conservation, is the most feasible and immediate action to alter the microwave programme with which we have chosen to cook the planet.

The theory is fine. But those trees will not include the Sumauma, or whale-tailed tree as I call it, that offers whole families shelter under the buttresses of its trunk, or in the warm, wardrobe-dark and -sized spaces between its roots. Such a slow-growing species, its ultimate immensity, and dare I say its individuality, would be impractical for the Greenhouse Forest. I stood under such a tree three days ago, fingering its bark, grey as the salt-burned trunks, dead as fossils, that are washed ashore on the beaches of my town. Its first tier of leaves high above the head looked red, then black against the hot white sky. Their frailty was confirmed by the carpet of dead vegetation under my feet.

And what was terrible, what was frightening, was the thought that trees might save us. They save us now, they save us every day. But it was terrible because we have forgotten the importance of trees and banished them from our minds. Two and a half million people depend on fuelwood for cooking and warmth. Every day the journeys by women and children to collect that wood become longer as the trees get scarcer. The Sumauma extended its pale limbs, the ground at my feet was thick with bursting gourds, great green and orange fruits that had fallen from nearby species. Their seeds, the size of beach pebbles, as dark and hard as jewels of anthracite, dried on the ground. Living without nature is our last art, and we are bringing it to a state of perfection. The petrol on the water was now only a faint purple stippling, the colour of a starling's feather. Plastic bottles, large as the gourds, rocked towards us in the tide.

The Greenhouse Forest would be our attempt at the ultimate technical solution. I think of the gloomy ranks of its dutiful broadleafs, the summary trials and executions in a state where it is a capital offence to harm a tree. But in this second another two acres fall, as M breastrokes out towards one of the islands, teasing me, the world's most firmly-committed non-swimmer, about the aquarium creatures she has glimpsed.

Unfortunately there is someone else aboard who goes one better. A brilliant diver, he returns to the surface clutching a large chunk of coral reef, submerges again, and reappears holding a star of the sea. This is an enormous orange starfish, like one of Voyager's images of the planet Saturn, he has prised from a rock. The looter looks up innocently for our applause, a mahogany statue in the surf.

Paying the skipper is the usual slow progress. Brazil's currency has changed twice in the past four years, and at its height inflation was running at 80 per cent per month. Old 'cruzeiro' notes are stamped with a 'cruzado' value which is already out of date. There are banknotes in circulation which are worth precisely nothing. Everyone, even the destitute in their cardboard hutches, or in the *favelas* on the hillsides of Rio, have their impressive wads of notes. But such bankrolls are the equivalent of a few pence. The skipper's an easy-going type. Noticing that we had brought no food for the long trip, he made his crew share with us the fried fish and manioc chips they had prepared on a fire on one of the beaches where we had waded ashore. The fish was enormous, its purple flesh of sawdust, its bones like javelins. Yet nothing I have tasted was so delicious. Up in the palms, the hunchbacked vultures are now the first brushstrokes of nightfall.

5

M is freaking out. In fact she is standing on the bed telling me the room has been invaded by armadillos. Knowing that is how she describes any creature over here larger than a mosquito, I am not immediately worried. This is a bit of a dive, I know. In fact the whole *pousada* is tropically dirty, but there is a shower, and air-conditioning that works. The eye of the fan, like that of a great yellow sunflower, follows us about the room.

But she is still panicking. The armadillos have shrunk a little, but fair play, these cockroaches are pretty well developed. They squat on the tiles, armoured like samurai. I remember once at home, coming downstairs at three in the morning. Two cockroaches, each as big as an engineer's thumb, were sitting side by side on the kitchen floor. They ticked like clocks, or the sound of a car cooling.

They live where there is dirt, I tell M. They eat dust like mini-hoovers, and are completely harmless. What's more, they are older than the dinosaurs, and can survive nuclear war, the nuclear winter, the neutron bomb, Star Wars, the hole in the ozone layer and the maddest contrivances of the greenhouse effect as if they were a mild case of cockroach influenza. We're sharing the room with the next dominant species on the planet. But to show her that for the moment at least 'Humans Rule O.K.' is still a credible slogan, I kick a few of the slower members of the tribe to pieces, and pursue the rest back to their crevices. It doesn't do much good. M stays awake all night, listening to the rustlings behind the wall, preparing for an invasion. The air-conditioner, loud as a helicopter in the room, accompanies her insomnia.

In the morning I can only console, but my satisfaction on encountering more of the state's wildlife is greeted with scornful silence. Outside on the verandah, the vampire bats we thought were escorting us back from a rather ripe restaurant turn out to be moths, bigger than my hand, arranged like museum displays against the wall. In fact the walk last night had been a curious journey. Toads the size of dinner-plates brayed in a nearby swamp. Along the sea-track between our *pousada* and the beach, luminous crabs had scuttled away from us, eyes on stalks. In the twilight they had looked like faint neon letters on some nightclub hoarding. Now we crunch across the sandy room away from our zoo. It is 9.15 a.m. and already 37° Centigrade.

Two hours later I am in academic mood. We are not tourists, I tell M, who has been foolish enough to use that derogatory word about ourselves. We are travellers, visitors, adventurers. We are experimenters. We are environmental pilgrims, discoverers, liaison-makers. We are pathfinders, trailblazers. We are definitely not tourists.

For my own self-esteem I repeat this litany as we sip sucos and watch a thunder storm flush out the polluted streets of a small fishing port. A meagre apparatus of maps and notebooks comforts more than the filaments of passion-fruit between my teeth.

Tourists are destroyers, I add firmly. Calling yourself a tourist is like fixing a satellite dish to the outside wall of your house. Or wearing a tee-shirt advertising a heavy metal group. Or going into a bar and ordering a lager and blackcurrant. It is admitting to membership of that empty-headed tribe that circulates the world leaving broken sandals and crumpled boxes of Kodachrome in its wake.

At home I can walk down a street and merge with its lobotomized current, passing Woolworths and Boots, Lo-Cost and Medicare. These stores contain exactly the same goods as the branches in the visitors' home towns. But here there's nothing to do but look at the familiar brands and imagine you're seeing something different. There's nothing to do and there's all day to do it in. So fourteen hours later the same sand-rashed, wild-eyed families are wandering the High Street, staring at displays of disposable nappies and pineapple chunks.

They are heroes, I suppose. They knew it was going to be undiluted hell, and they still came. They came in coaches with their neighbours. They came in cars with their in-laws and friends. They came grimly resolved to enjoy themselves, muttering that this time, this time of all the times, this time would be a good time. And that makes them heroes. In my book it makes them almost as heroic as the ones that stayed home.

Our town would die without tourists. And tourists are killing our town. I can't walk down the street or buy a stamp without encountering an immovable battalion of their infantry engaged in the slow murder of our town. Thank Christ you're here, I want to say. At last you've arrived! We couldn't have held out much longer. We couldn't have survived without you. We were down to our last tea-towel that tells you all the castles to visit. And the frozen, takeaway pizzas in their yellow plastic boxes, you know, the ones you like to use as frisbees. They were nearly all gone. So thank Christ you've come. And out into the street we go, at tourist speed. Which is the speed of bewilderment. The speed with which the icicles of limestone lengthen in the bonking bunkers under the sea wall. The speed of discovery that you are irredeemably lost in the shadowlands, the territory of ruin, the Tolkeinscape of dereliction between Woolworths and the piss-coloured cement of the promenade.

Which is at least a speed more dynamic than that achieved by the cars we overtake, each a hutch of pink-eyed, hamster-cheeked warring sects. We trudge past the stationary traffic and feel almost absolved. The town is car-blitzed, car-wrecked. The town is insane with cars. It is car-stupid, car-fucked. They stretch for miles into the distance under their roof of blue, corrosive exhaust. They want to come in but there's no room left. Can't they see there's a 'No Vacancies' sign written in nitrous oxide over our peninsula?

£25,000 worth of German steel and teak veneer is immobilised behind a fourteen year-old caravanette, garnishing with lead, with murderous carbon monoxide the ripening orchards at the side of the road. With pushchairs, with supermarket trolleys heaped with the yellow howitzer-shells of Australian lager cans, with sunburn and aorta-toughening stress, we overtake the rust-acned Cortinas, the juddering Ladas. And for the first time in the day we can feel good about ourselves. For the first time at home we can enjoy the tourist scene.

But here we are not tourists, I tell M. Rio was hysterical with cars. It had overdosed on the methedrine of cars. But we were not tourists there when we sat in the bars of Ipanema and watched the surfers combing the salt out of each other's hair. We were not tourists when we stood outside the chained and shuttered nightclub owned by Ronald Biggs in Copacabana. Someone should break in, M suggested reasonably, and knock the little bastard over the head. And we were not tourists when we sat alone in a cathedral-sized cinema, hugging our knees as the air-conditioning started to bite, entranced by the American hoodoo, the lonely cult of English words.

Anyway, I calculate, Brazil's too big for us to hurt. It's two and a half times the size of India and a zillion times bigger than Wales. We can't touch it, we can't leave a trace. But I think of the strange Antarctica of sand at Saquerema. We had walked miles out of town and the beach had become an endless white dune. There was not a mark on it, not a coke can, a fishing hook, a crushed pack of Hollywoods. We looked back over the prehistoric landscape and saw two lines of footprints running up to meet us in the seamless, the creaking sand. We had walked for miles where no-one else had ever trod, and there were our signatures on the canvas to prove it. We were the first, and we were the only ones.

We were not tourists there, and neither are we here, watching the floods wash the litter and the shit into the sea, counting our rainbows of currency. On a television in the corner the President is speaking. He looks young enough to be a rock star making a comeback. And he has just done something devastating to our money. It means we have only half the amount we thought we possessed. I suck at an immovable shred of passion-fruit and watch the crowds return to the bank outside. Their queue quickly reforms after the cloudburst, and the army, with guns and sticks, re-emerges too. The soldiers, in little blue-shirted knots, allow only two people into the bank at a time. Meanwhile, the television says that in Sao Paulo, the supermarkets have been looted. Prices go up as reflation starts to act. Suddenly our beautiful grey and green dollars aren't buying so much.

The 'cruzado novo' is making a comeback. We thought it had been hit for six, that it was on its back out of the ring. But the emaciated, the ashamed new cruzado is giving the dollar, and the dollar's little butty, the pound sterling, a bit of a pasting. The people don't understand it, so they loot the supermarkets. We don't understand it, so we watch them do it. The moneychangers don't understand it. When I visit a jeweller or travel agent to make a transaction – these are also black market currency dealers – they offer me ridiculous, impossible sums.

When I protest, they shrug. The Brazilians have a language of shrugs. Their shrugs have an infinite variety. Today in the jeweller's the shrug I received came with an X certificate. It was an 18 plus, adults only, take-it-or-leave-it-and-if-you-leave-it-I-couldn't-give-a-fuck-type shrug. If you could write that shrug it would have an immediate paperback edition.

So we sit with our inky columns of Brazilian mathematics and watch President Collor explain his enormous experiment with the economy. Of course we don't understand a word he says, but the talking heads of the O Globo media empire are giving it an immediate and detailed post-mortem.

But you don't need to speak the language to know that Brazil is pleased with its president. And that it is also slightly amazed, slightly awed by Collor. The man is going places and he wants to take the country with him. It is not that he is, or looks, young. Brazil is a young country. Half its population is under twenty. Astonishingly, a quarter of its people are under ten. And it is not that Collor has unpolitical good looks. There are so many Brazilians that a good face, a fine face on the banknotes or the medals is no big deal. What is interesting about Collor is his capacity for the unexpected. His choice of advisers and ministers draws bigger headlines than the Brazilian soccer defeat at Wembley stadium.

The referee is a thief, the headlines bawl. The referee is a crook and the one-nil scoreline a catastrophic travesty, claims the authoritative pink broadsheet hung at every news-stand, between the zeppelin-like pricks of the gay soft-core monthlies and the latest pictures of Paul McCartney's world tour. For Collor is pushing the universal standbys of sport and sex and telly slightly to the wings. His appointment, for example, of José Lutzenberger, as environment minister, is a sensational gesture. The newsprint gasps. Because Lutzenberger is green. Lutzenberger is seriously green. Lutzenberger is so seriously green that he is the world's most respected environmentalist. And his speciality is the Amazonian rainforest. And now he has a favoured place at the side of the Brazilian president.

On television, Lutzenberger looks as he normally does. Square-jawed, determined, dressed-down. He sits surrounded by the other ministers and advisors, by men in suits, by men in splendid military uniforms, by men unreadable behind dark glasses, by men with polished holsters and riding crops. He looks outnumbered and outgunned, but he has now achieved a position where he might conceivably make a difference to the process of survival of this planet. But he has also attained a prominence that can affect the monies earned from the rainforest by cattle ranchers, land owners, mine owners, estate barons. And the rainforest oligarchies can watch him on television and decide whether what he says is permissible. (In the first burning-season since Lutzenberger's appointment, the fires in the eastern Amazon, at least, seem as great as ever.)

Television is important in Brazil, and it's grim. Was it last night, or the night before, we spent two hours as the hot rains fell, watching pulp American horror mess up the screen. Men with chainsaws. Women with radioactive lipstick. The green-tinged undead breaking the surface of autumnal crypts. The usual American mixture of psychopaths and relentless self-pity. There are lots of channels here and lots of sets. Even in the slums, the real slums, the people without water and toilets, without clothes and privacy, without decent food or the hope of getting out, possess TV. Even in the *favelas* there is television, a bristling of aerials, a trade in big colour jobs, in fuzzy portables. Or should I say, especially in the *favelas* there is television. As especially in the *favelas* there are drugs, and police executions of the seven, the eight year-old couriers of cocaine and all its counterfeits. As also in the *favelas* there is malnutrition, typhoid, the exchange of deadly spores. But especially in the *favelas* there is television.

What's important is that we don't judge the country by the dubbed grotesqueries of its late night schedules. What's important, I suppose, is that we don't judge the country at all. But it's tempting to label Brazil, to ticket the place, when the weather makes you tired, hungover and unambitious, in some steamed up *lanchonete*, and the early morning TV is in full swing.

Then you can make your feeble assumptions about the state of its cultures as you watch Xuxa emerge from her rocket-ship, her gleaming space-oyster, and parachute into the ruthlessly-cranked hysteria of her fans. Xuxa is the empress of children's television, and the most famous person in Brazil. She is tall and blonde, with skin of flawless Nordic silk. She is the queen of kiddies' television and her audience is 75 per cent adult.

Xuxa descends from her temple with its nuclear reactor somewhere in the clouds, and a ruffled minion presents her with an enormous golden platter of tropical fruits. She takes a grape, one delicate berry, and places it carefully in her mouth. The corral of chaos around her, the leaping children, the swaying dancers, seems to calm for an instant. It is a holy moment when Xuxa eats. And then Xuxa is talking, she is singing, she is dancing, and the madness begins again.

Of course, anyone familiar with children's TV in Britain or America will know the formula. A stage tribe of nine and ten year-olds is kept locked in the studio for a week and fed nothing but tartrazine and concentrations of E numbers. Then they are given a pep talk by the programme director that would make a mullah's call for revolutionary holy war sound like a Radio Three weather forecast. And it's these kids that make up Xuxa's army, her gang of milk-toothed, soprano devotees that jive on skateboards, climb ropes and trample each other underfoot as she makes her space-pharaoh's progress through two hours of Brazilian prime time.

There are books about Xuxa at every news-stand. Her latest record shows only her head, her Venusian face, above the petal-sprinkled surface of a swimming pool. Her new video reveals more of her alien's beauty. She poses heart-stoppingly in a costume of asterisks, in her intergalactic underwear. Fathers in Rio buy the books and tapes for their children, and whistle her hits uncertainly, unwillingly, as they crush into the buses speeding in from Niteroi, from Barra. These are the songs they are not supposed to know.

6

Off Avenida Rio Branco the hawkers are offering the death of Chico Mendes on tee-shirts. A crude red and green design shows a forest of tree stumps with a dead man sprawled beneath them, his name emblazoned on his back like that of some designer tracksuit maker. As in the west, Mendes has become famous since his death, a figure of environmental mythology. And the greater his fame the more numbing the myth, the more difficult it is for others to follow his example.

He was a brave man who believed in the dignity and importance of the work of his fellow rubber tappers. He was aware of the destruction of the rainforest, and believed that only careful, controlled exploitation, as practised by the rubber tapping industry, could save it. Vague Western hopes of freezing the rainforests in time, after first banishing the gold miners, the cattle barons and all the other ecological villains were impossibly sentimental. The forest, Mendes knew, was a place where people worked, lived and died, and could never be that arcadia or enormous, unconfined nature park that suburbanites had tried to fantasize into reality.

Of course the rainforest is important to the West for psychological reasons. Forget for a moment, if that is possible (it certainly is not wise) that its products contribute vital ingredients to a quarter of our medical prescriptions. Put aside the fact that vast quantities of the foods and drinks we take for granted (the domestic hen is descended from two species of jungle fowl) originate there. We desire the tropical rainforests to exist because of our very lack of knowledge of what they contain. We need them because they constitute some of the last places on the planet that have not been visited or explored.

Thus they still might harbour the strange and miraculous, the very unknown that our souls crave, as we tread once more the too familiar trackways of our own existences. And the people that might yet be found in those areas of forest, uncontacted, nameless, are surely the inhabitants of our dreams, men and women of limitless potential, unconstricted by everything that confines us to the mundane. We need their savage gentleness, the reality of their remote survival along with all the other extraordinary untouched wealth of the uncharted forests. Anything might exist, be possible, in that dark green territory of the unconscious.

Some fantasies are worth having, as long as we do not blame the world for not offering them to us as a reality. And despite the images of the malaria-ravaged Yanomami, the largest warrior tribe of Brazil, brought after twenty thousand years to squalid subjection and the brink of extinction, we will persist in seeing the rainforest as that psychological dark side of the moon, which somehow might offer to us personally, the secret we have misplaced and now hunt for through our dreams.

Taking an outside table at the restaurant in Copacabana was perhaps a mistake. But it's too hot to be inside, and even from here I can see the young roaches waving their brown arms as they cross the walls above the customers' heads. Those dark limbs remind me of the *abandonados* on the beach, the deserted children of four or five who must beg to live. Incredibly – I still cannot quite credit the statistic – one in eleven of the Brazilian population of 135 million is an abandoned child. I came here believing the plight of the Amazonian Indians was the greatest crisis in this country. Suddenly and uncomfortably, I am having to rethink.

Even on our very modest and tentative explorations, we have discovered that the rainforest is not the colourful world that we have displayed on our tee-shirts. Rather it is green, dark, impenetrable and entirely unwelcoming. Nor does it teem with cuddly jaguars and toucans. Instead there is a silence, what appears to our untutored eyes and ears as an ominous lack of life. And neither are the Indians the noble innocents we had imagined. Instead they are suffering the consequences, like the *abandonados* and all the other destitute people on the streets of Rio and Sao Paulo, of Brazil's monstrous international debt. The country owes a cool 110 billion dollars to the West. When we talk of foreign aid, we neglect the fact that in interest payments alone, Brazil gives us far more than we are able to offer. It is poverty that is destroying the rainforest, exactly as it is dulling the minds and crippling the bodies of the orphans on Avenida Princesa Isabel who now approach our restaurant table.

Because the Third World is being looted. In 1989 alone its countries handed over 30 billion dollars to their creditors, most of whom were western banks, insured against failure of such payments. The countries paid up by cutting health and education spending, by allowing environmental destruction to proceed for short-term profit. If debtor countries like Brazil renege on their payments, there will be no economic calamity in the West. Vast sums known as 'provisions' have been set aside against such possible loss. Yet the policy remains to exact as much repayment as possible. A woman comes past carrying a bundle. She wears a ragged purple tee-shirt, the English words 'we can dream' emblazoned over her breasts. I feel for the bankroll in my pocket, unpeel a few of the multi-coloured, almost worthless notes used here for small change. But the woman has gone.

And perhaps it is now, spreading the murky greens and reds of the wad before us, that we have the small idea that some months later, on the field of the greatest cultural festival of a country six thousand miles away, we will use this money as a symbol of what the West is doing to Brazil.

The snouts of the television cameras are lowered into the attaché case to devour the rainbow of Brazilian cash. Neatly placed in bundles over a bed of photocopies, it seems there might be a considerable fortune here. This is the occasion of the National Eisteddfod of Wales, taking place in a mining area that has haemorrhaged money for the last one hundred and fifty years. Coal created wealth, that, wherever it circulated, never stayed in the drab terraces and pit villages of this valley.

A group of young people with the attaché case opened, and bearing enormous cheques that state in the Welsh language, that they are paying back Third World Debt to the UK's four major high street banks, visit the public relations marquees of Lloyds, Barclays, National Westminster and Midland. On the field, the eisteddfod visitors are urged to have their own cheques marked with the imperative slogan 'Stamp Out Debt Not the Rainforests'. Each cheque bearing that slogan is an atom of pressure in the campaign. Smart, polite and monumentally non-committal, the bank officials listen to our explanations and gently refuse our attempt to make a deposit on behalf of the Brazilian poor, on behalf of the young crone in the purple tee shirt who is now not even a speck in the crowd.

Hopeless idealism, but the cameras devour it. Perhaps it is the novelty of the idea that money might be distributed more equally that attracts them. For Brazil has unimaginable wealth. It has the money smell. At a drinks shack, listening to rain beat the corrugated sheeting, watching the ochre dirt road outside begin to slide past, I breathe in that smell. At a street corner where a legless man begs for food, and a mother screens her sleeping child from the afternoon's 100°F., I inhale that dark green smell. It is the musk of flower-water, cloudy in urns, the lotion of sunbathers remote behind dark glasses, as they join a bus queue. It is the parched upholstery of a car, its doors opening like the blades of a jack-knife. It is the flesh of gourds, honeycombed by ants, crushed in a gutter. The stores sell gold and precious stones. On a bed of velvet a trunk of purple rock has been split to reveal crystals the size of pheasant eggs. And everywhere I have turned today, darker-skinned now and lighter of hair, fairer in fact than I have been for twenty years, authentic in vest and ragged shorts, the moneychangers have lined me up for their fusillade of languages, pleading, warning, threatening.

On our last day today we visited the small Manhattan of Rio Sul, the cavernous, smoked-glass shopping mall. The music is American easy-listening. Which means it is very, very difficult to listen to without wanting to commit an act of violence. The light is the colour of the transparent lozenges of violet soap found in expensive hotel bathrooms. The air is an explosion of frost as you cross the threshold. We walked there through the Copacabana tunnel, a quarter mile of darkness and diesel fumes left by the squadrons of buses heading for Botofago and the Centro. At the far end of the tunnel a woman crouched above an oil drum, stirring chicken skins in bubbling fat. Beyond her, the candle-sellers waited under tarpaulins and broken parasols, their trays of tallow and plastic statuary blocking the pavement. Behind them the ornate gates of the church were locked, but hung with assembly-line images of saints. Two children played in the dust with a lizard they had captured, whilst all the time the diesel-filled air writhed at the tunnel mouth like a genie.

A man offered to clean my shoes, gesturing to a tall seat, a man with one brown tooth and a torso tight as a clenched fist. The shoeshine chair would hold me high above his head as he blacked my heel-less Clarks. It was an ornate, over-complicated contraption of dark polished wood, and reminded me of a baby's high-stool. As the lizard's tail snapped off like a piece of lego I stepped over the invisible barrier, and the doors of Rio Sul opened obediently. Its cool scarves of air wound themselves over the dust and traffic burns I carried in from the already forgotten street.

Now at our table we finger a blue parrot bought in a nearby store. Painstakingly and ingeniously woven from coloured threads, we perch it on a chairback and from a few yards away it looks entirely lifelike. I especially admire its large red glass eye that seems to follow the progress of beggars up the street, the hustlers selling sweets and gum and Coke.

There should be a tee-shirt design here that says 'Buy a Coke, Save a life'. In fact I'm surprised the Coca Cola Corporation hasn't thought of it already. But if I had to design a shirt, that's the slogan

I'd put on it. Thank Christ for the grinding heat here, for international thirst. I give my pennies, swill the drink, and the child, the old woman who has sold me the bottle might be able to start work again in the morning.

Now the limousines pull up outside the onyx pinnacle of the Meridien. The anonymously wealthy, the anonymously famous slip into the elevators and up to their pools and catalogues of hotel pornography. Next to the hotel I watch a fire-eater blow ostrich feathers of yellow flame across the street. He pauses, rinses his mouth with something from a Coke bottle, and breathes out another plume, a delicate, violet-coloured tongue of energy. The man is naked but for a pair of soot-stained shorts. His fire corkscrews across the street, over the restaurant tables of the diners, towards the beach where a floodlit soccer game is taking place. I suck my cheeks. What do you do with such pointless magic, how do you use that talent. Under the hoardings, the size of buses that advertize the arrival of British rock-stars in Brazil, people are curling up to sleep. They are tucking their children under car-bonnets and rubbish sacks as the rest of the city starts to come alive.

The match on the beach draws a crowd. Two barefoot teams in immaculate kit skate across a surface that this morning sapped the spring from my legs after only two hundred yards' slow trudge. The sand has cooled now, from the molten broth of noon, and has been raked, but is still wrinkled by deep furrows and undulations. But the players touch only the surface, as if it was the delicately nurtured and irrigated grass of the Maracana that hosted their game.

The crowd grows bigger. Like them I am watching one man. Of the twenty-two quick and skilful players on the sand, there is one who has the power to mesmerize. Of all the chauffeurs and waiters, the bus drivers and cooks on the pitch, a balding, unshaven, thirtyish number 10 in the Greens keeps us watching. Makes us watch. Older than the rest, he gets blown more quickly. He is the only one who shows agony, real pain, when he loses the ball or misdirects a pass. Not that he makes many errors, but it's worth it to see him stop and raise his face to heaven, eyes screwed up tight, and murmur silent oaths. But it's what he tries and how often he succeeds that fascinate. The flicks, the swerves, the overheads, the outrageous frauds. Once, he takes the ball on his chest, bounces it on his thigh, and volleys it thirty yards across the pitch to his strikers, both of whom are too amazed at the impetuosity, the bravado, to make anything of the opportunity. He rubs a sandy instep and smiles in disdain.

When he is substituted, early in the second half, I start to lose interest, watching the game, still furiously paced, over my shoulder. The shoeshine artists are out, pitching their impressive, backside-polished high-chairs at the very edge of the sand. An Indian, bristling with feathers, wanders down the avenida. His high Asian cheeks are painted orange as toucan bills. Far away now, like a pale bud of flame, the fire-eater is hissing into the dusk.

Beggars who this morning squatted on street corners and traffic islands are still there. The red lights are long on this boulevard. They give time for a young man with one leg and a crutch to hop into the stationary traffic and ask for money. Some drivers roll up their windows, others hand over a few notes. Some stare straight ahead and ignore the opened palm twitching before them. Then the light turns green and the young man vaults back to the grassy central reservation, where he is met by another. There is some sort of an argument and the cripple throws down the crumpled ball of cruzados and moves off to sit on a bollard. The second man retrieves the money and when the lights turn red, the beggar is out again, tapping at the windows of cars.

We have prioritized Brazil's crises. The rainforest is the world's genetic reservoir. Its destruction will affect our climate, health and future. The Indian cultures are curious, attractive and present real lessons. But the urban poor seem to have no culture to offer us. Their world is merely the grisly underside of our own. They are unfortunate losers, whilst the tribes of the Amazon are blameless victims. So we look straight into dark, liquid eyes. The kids point at our plates, shamefully heaped in the way only Brazilians and Americans know how, and then at the plastic bags they carry. These two, it seems, are begging for others. We put rice and bread and meat into their hands, mixing with everything else they have scrounged in the restaurant. They cross the road to a traffic island and start to share out the spoils. Meanwhile, outside a *boite*, a strip-joint, and beneath a TV screen that shows a version of the cabaret inside, a mother puts her child to sleep on the pavement. When men cluster round the monitor they drop their cruzados into her lap. The baby, dark and naked, stares up serenely at the sky.

The Scheme of Things

A nd you know if you've worked in the last nine months you're probably illegible for this job?'

My partner on the interviewing panel put this question twelve times in two hours as the candidates trooped into the Job Centre cubicle. The twelve men, all between eighteen and twenty-five, nodded or smiled. They didn't speak much, but stared about at the total blankness of the room. Police stations were friendlier. From the corridor we could hear the whirring of a photocopier as we processed the true and fabricated details of their lives. By the end of the afternoon we'd cut the national unemployment figure by ten.

Two weeks later we were five miles away in the middle of a wood. Rain bounced like pebbles off the shed's roof, and in front of the gas-heater waterproofs and orange overalls threw up a curtain of steam. The ten strangers had already fallen into easy comradeship, leaning together like their muddied tools outside. They were going to spend a year in this place, a windy peninsula of beaches, cliffs and salt-poisoned trees. And above these was their site for working and training, a dynamited and bulldozed castle, its ruins almost invisible in the grass. In other words these young men were beginning a Community Programme scheme, three days a week, £2.10 an hour, find your own food and transport, no other employment allowed. Below us in a large walled area of Victorian gardens was another shed. Here a group of younger men on a different scheme played brag and waited for the typhoon to abate. The only difference in their accommodation was the walls, covered to the floor with pictures of girls flung into poses of hurt, pleading and synthetic ecstasy. In the half-light the mosaic of these photographs resembled a murky stained glass.

No one seemed to mind at first the barrowing, digging, turf- and brick-laying. It filled the time and generated an appetite. The castle existed only on creased, inaccurate documents, but the views were still aristocratically wide. You might have been able to see right round the belly of the Glamorgan coast, and standing on the cliff-tops you looked down on gulls floating like lunch-wrappings on and off the ledges. For much of the time the area was deserted. In summer the beaches would fill with thousands of trippers, but for half the year at least, walkers and occasional school parties were the only visitors.

So the members of the scheme quickly began to impress themselves upon the life of the peninsula. There was Phil, mechanic with yard-long hair, who disappeared after eight months to tinker with engines on the fated Peace Convoy in Wiltshire. Mike was another who wanted to work, singing in Welsh as he smoothed the turves down on a new bank, leaning his whole body against the damp grass. And there was Bylo, whose talent was story-telling. I suppose he made the winter memorable with various excerpts from his autobiography. Whoring in the army stews in Germany, stealing peregrine eggs, and once on a coach trip with his soccer club to the Isle of Wight, holding up a post office with a gun made of newspaper. I visited him at home several times. He lived in a hilltop village twelve miles from work on an estate usually wrapped in saturating mist. Behind the house floes of sitka covered the mountainside, while on the scrap of lawn in front a Marina chassis was jacked on bricks. Inside, brothers, sisters and alsatians tumbled about in front of a video, and Bylo would come downstairs, muzzy from a noon sleep. Digging had become pointless. He'd curse the futility of travelling to a filthy shed for wages that provided an existence but no life. And if you didn't work there was no money and he had the 'flu. There was a better living selling tabs in the club or poaching forestry deer. He showed me his wage slips where the take-home was shrunk to a pittance by deductions for absence and weeks of emergency tax. One of the last times I saw him he was digging in the sodden earth of the Victorian gardens. Blurred and silly after taking acid the night before, he was still talking about army life and soccer trips and the daughter he could never visit. I think he was twenty-two years old.

One by one they dropped out of the scheme, but were easily re-placed. Prison and detention centres claimed a few, or sometimes another job turned up. The others finally found travelling down to the isolated coast too expensive. Often there were protests about the nature of the work, but sometimes an unadmitted pleasure as a long promenade of liverish Victorian brick was recreated, and the squat quoins of the castle rose out of the excavations. Gradually the standard council-issue clothes were dispensed with for another uniform of mutilated denim and steel-tipped boots. As the rain fell, they'd spend mornings cruising in battered Sherpas through the maze of country lanes around the site, nominally on errands for sand or cement, but really killing time, the full volume of the transistor the only sound between miles of wet hedgerows.

In breaks of the atrocious weather there would be other expeditions. Some of the boys would take their syrupy tea and Mother's Pride down to a beach of raised limestone eroded to the intricacy of track at a railway terminus. Here they ate or sunbathed around pools fringed with rosebud-like sea anemones and the bleaching husks of crabs. Over the cliffs a waterfall dropped directly to the sand, concealing the triangular mouth of a cave. If it hadn't been for the sea's trapped, urinous stench, this might have made a good place for an undiscoverable doss. Inside, the rocks possessed a muscular roundness, the surface offering resistance to the tides that yet managed to wedge into roof and walls milk crates, childrens' spades and detergent bottles. I always felt there was something admirable, though sinister, in plastic's refusal to decay or even corrode. It lay around us on that remote beach as a puzzling natural phenomenon. High tides and storms always brought this home. When the waves retreated, the beaches, picnic areas, streams and roads around the coast looked like the site of a pop festival. Great sheets of polythene the colour of seawater lay shredded on the rocks. Traffic bollards were found embedded in the newly-exposed sand, while a knotted gout of condoms like a baby octopus would usually be discovered slithering round the disabled-parking zone. And a strange frost would lie over the beach. Even in summer it might seem from a distance that the tide had left a delicately frozen world behind it. On closer inspection the ice comprised granules of polystyrene that float in the waters of the Bristol Channel like some inedible plankton. The boys would brush up all this rubbish and shovel it into pick-ups for dumping inland. In a throw-away society they were the ones who'd spend most of their work-time wading through other people's trash. And the next big tide would bring in similar cargoes as the sea coughed the muck out of its lungs.

In winter the cold stopped us dead. Soil became an anvil, the waterfall that pounded the beach grew solid as a column of sweating marble. But in the shed the talk would be brewing up. Nick, who could never actually work, because of a massive daily dose of tranquillizers, described his dance classes and singing lessons. Most of his money went on training to be a star. Everyone said he was one already as he discoed in fermenting daps over the spilled cement. Alun talked about September when the scheme finished and he would take up an engineering place in university, being the passport to the big bread. Meanwhile the diligent Mike would finger the latest rip in his jacket and mumble that it was a legacy from the barbed wire on a grocery shop's back window. That was said to be Mike's problem. He was tempted by things that belonged to other people. Tools, videos, even coal, were offered round the site at knock-down prices. Whenever he didn't come into work we'd wait for his mother's apologetic call that he was 'down the station' again. But his excellent probation officer, and the references I concocted that made him sound like a cross between Robin Hood and a Barnardo boy, kept him out of prison until a month before the scheme ended.

The weather frustrated everything except these talks. They were the mortar that kept the group together, the rough friction of strong characters who some days liked and other days hated each other. At the interviews I'd promised a summer of lunchtime swimming and sunbathing. Twenty-four days in August it rained, and the yews and evergreen oaks around the shed dripped like the days' sullen conversation. But there were other times. On a scorching noon they'd lie with backs against the glazed brick of the vinery and watch geology students picnic out of pastel-coloured knapsacks. Parties of pensioners would stroll around the shrubberies, then come down to the office to protest about the workmen's language and manic soccer spoiling a peaceful afternoon. They must have looked an intimidating group, provoking each other with jagged nicknames and flying clods, their tattoos like images of derision for less spectacular lives.

So in the heat or eye-watering cold they'd stand on the summit of the peninsula, sifting the fruitless rubble for traces of the original buildings. Broken tiles and glass and porcelain were all that turned up. On the first day the boys had been given a lecture on the history of their work site. People had lived here since the Bronze Age; there was a Silurian fort that had been photographed from the air. The Romans might have attacked the place, and the Saxons definitely did. And Edward VIII had taken a dip in the bay around the corner. 'If we find any treasure we're keeping it,' Bylo had said. 'It's the only bloody way we'll get rich down here.' And the digging went on. Very carefully Alun would place hazard markers around the pits he had dug. Nick, perspiring violently, would knock them over. Of course, they never completed the work they had been hired for. Inheriting what looked like chaos from the previous year's scheme, they left behind half-finished pathways, blunt tools and flat batteries. Perhaps their papers have already gone through the county council shredder, but with the qualification of another year's unemployment, some of them might wish to return to the coast and that windy promontory. It had its moments. Sometimes as they slogged with mattocks and spades, a group of trippers, loaded with all the slightly embarrassing paraphernalia of organized leisure, would stop and ask what they were doing. And Mike, on his knees with a trowel, would squint up at the question. 'It's a castle,' he'd say, digging into the compo, balancing just the right amount on the blade. 'Look lovely when it's finished.'

Our Back Pages

The pitch, as ever, resembled a paddyfield ploughed by bison. There were rumours that the school sewage pipes ran directly beneath it, and having fractured years previously, contributed to the perennial ooze. Despite such hazards, I had remained remarkably unstained by either ground or the opposing team. Loitering on the wing, all I had done during seventy-five minutes of the match was throw the ball into innumerable line-outs and immediately retreat to one of the few green islands in the slime. After four years in secondary school I had still not adjusted to the practicalities of large-scale team games. I came from a primary so small even a noughts-and-crosses competition needed a casting director of the deepest ingenuity. Rugby was not even dreamt about.

My jersey remained an advert for the local laundry; I could even distinguish the colours of the hooped socks. In the middle of the field the sixteen forwards, teams and identities interchangeable, clung to one another in some mysterious rite. The ball was nowhere to be seen. There were one or two spectators of course. Whatever the weather there was always someone bored or desperate enough to come out of the nearby streets and watch a schoolboys' game. Furtively I smeared a handful of earth over my right knee and up the leg of my alarmingly white shorts. I had to look as if I had made some contribution to the proceedings, and mud in this contest was the badge of suffering and endeavour. I was so pleased with the result that I was soon caressing my other leg and massaging, sunbather-like, the too-obvious scarlet of my jersey shoulder. The shouted warnings came too late. I looked up and the opposing threequarters were moving for the first time in the match. The ball had reached the outside centre and he was bearing down with what, even now, seems indecent haste. I took one step out of my quagmire and he was gone, a blue flash, an agonized expression narrowing his brow and twisting his mouth.

That look remains vivid. I can shut my eyes and yet not avoid the centre's ugly determination and ridiculous self-belief. Didn't he know it was only a game, the barmy sod, as he hurled me into the marsh and kneed me in the stomach for good measure. He was the type who started shaving before he was fifteen and pissed over you in the shower. And now the bastard had gone and scored a try.

I hate rugby. I detest it as a Christian fundamentalist might a primitive tribal religion – with a mixture of pity and horrified fascination for those who still labour under the influence of the old, grotesque gods. But it's not the players who bring out this loathing. They seem a reasonable, if misguided set of lads. Thugs, yes, but decent thugs – apart from the policemen, that is, who now bring the tactics of picket-bashing and the midnight knock increasingly into the sport.

Rather, it's the whole Welsh rugby ethos and massive establishment importance of the game in this country that provoke this feeling. And the hatred finds its climax on International days. You always know when these games are due because the *Western Mail* suddenly grows twenty-five pages fatter than usual. Its battery of rugby writers, far larger than its political and arts staff combined, become sporting archaeologists. Old games are replayed in newsprint, ancient highlights relived, past 'heroes' compared with modern 'stars'. The whole process of build-up, International and subsequent analysis, lasts about two weeks. If Wales win, the celebration takes the unique form of prolonged national gloating and a long immersion in the warm bath of self-congratulation. And if the Welsh team loses there is the immediate and hilarious country-wide hunt for scapegoats and excuses, and then the generation of an atmosphere of blame and near-suicidal depression. Superstars return to the status of honest mediocrities. Journalists grow wise on the secrets of hindsight. But what is most terrifying is the way all energy and dynamism in the country seem sucked into the morass of the International game. Rugby then becomes completely unavoidable, and even those hard-cases who thought they had renounced the sport and all its superstitions forever, feel the poisoned gene of inherited Saturday-Welshness suddenly playing up. Look at the faces of those honest family men who spend International afternoons where most sane British folk are to be found on such occasions: at the Garden Centre, the DIY Superstore and the Leisure Park. They twitch with an old addiction, are sad with vague but unvanquishable longing. And there's always some saboteur with a transistor to tell them we've just been stuffed by the All Blacks or Tonga to crown a perfect day.

If the Welsh neurosis is our constant search for heroes, sport and especially rugby provide our richest heroic seam. Most recently it is the outside-half, Jonathan Davies, who has been poxed by our strange love. The sporting press, with its extraordinary cabbalistic vocabulary, made him saviour, wizard, magician. He would dance on a pin-head, and somehow, by the workings of an unspecified but indisputable genius, inspire victory. Thus when he played like a mortal the tribal elders were confused. The rainmaker had not made rain: the gods seemed unfriendly. So the rituals were intensified and public sacrifice introduced. Davies escaped the 'axe', but the old king, David Pickering, copped it in the neck. Yet at least he has the chance to get on with real life. That other Welsh hero, boxer Johnny Owen, ended beaten, brain-damaged, then dead, professionally executed in Los Angeles in 1981. Many will remember the build-up to that contest, and the way all our front and back pages exploited the 'Owen phenomenon'. The 'Merthyr matchstick-man' with his chance of fame and wealth and above all, sporting deification, was seen as a tonic for a country beset by strikes, unemployment and national anaemia. So Wales nudged him into an arena where he never belonged. We gave him a decent burial of course, but the general, unspoken view was that Owen had failed. And in public too. So you don't hear much about him in the recycling industry of sporting myth. He's an embarrassment.

For others, this process works in reverse. Carwyn James was a player, then a tactician and coach. He was also a minor politician, a college lecturer and a civilized human being, but those are not the type of things that make a man famous in Wales. He died prematurely a few years ago and since then a distinguished body of writers has transformed his common-or-garden 'legendary' status into sainthood. Every trifling memoir of the man appears in stained-glass prose. We have washed him in sentimentality and embalmed him with hazy, largely inaccurate memories of famous tours and victories. We do this because the country (not the people) has a vampire-like craving for heroes, living or dead, invented or slightly less imaginary. And what is peculiar is that some of the best modern Welsh writers, when dealing with this subject, lurch immediately into cliché, usually of a religious nature. Thus Alun Richards produced a history of Welsh rugby called *A Touch of Glory*, while Dai Smith and Gareth Williams planted *Fields of Praise*. And the long-lamented (by this reader at any rate) *Arcade* nearly capsized itself with a first issue designed to look and read as a high-brow International programme.

Despite what the media make of rugby in Wales and the elevation of jockstrap culture to some form of high-art ceremonial, despite the debenture-selling industry and the large sections of our 'National Ground' annexed by big business, most of the spectators have the correct idea about International games. They provide the platforms for some of the world's great drinking festivals. It's booze not rugby that provides escape, excitement and oblivion on those fervent Saturdays. Rugby is merely an excuse, like Christmas, for getting sozzled. Which is fine, though the habit of our historians in defining the game as the major social experience of working class, industrial South Wales, can be irritating. There is now only one working-class Welsh team game and that is the consumption of alcohol. Everything else, like rugby, baseball, pigeons or mouse-training is minor in popular appeal or merely provides a framework for demonstrations of a drinking talent. And as International crowds grow increasingly remote from the chapel hymnology and Welsh language of the past and take to pop songs or the mindless 'Here We Go' incantation, as the myths of hwyl become exposed as beer-fuelled fevers of maudlin frustration, we will learn perhaps to accept the fact that our sporting culture is a drinking culture, and after eight pints anyone can play a dummy scissors and go over in the corner. I spoke to Ioan, aged seventeen, from Pontypridd about one of the Welsh home games this season. He and a friend had arrived in Cardiff at 9am. By 10.30 they had finished a bottle of rum and were in the queue at the 'Old Arcade'. Although they owned tickets, both had decided to sell them and watch the match on a video screen at a local hotel. It was always a fantastic day out, said Ioan. He'd looked forward to it the whole season. I liked Ioan immediately. He knew what international rugby was all about.

I had no such precision of thought when I was that age. In fact I was only then managing to free myself from the tyranny of organised team games, which brings me to my second and final memory of playing. As usual I was loitering without intention on the wing when the opposing outside-half aimed a monstrous punt into my pleasantly untroubled area of the field. He was a member of that most dreaded of all Welsh institutions, a 'rugby family', and in fact was the younger brother of J.P.R. Williams, built like a Toby jug and sporting a blond crew-cut cruel as razorblades. The ball grew tiny as a satellite, then dropped, to my astonishment, cleanly into my hands. Looking up I found myself in space. There was nobody within twenty yards and the opposing team's try-line lay a short sprint away. No one stood between me and a historic winning score. A shout went up from a few sodden spectators. I had visions of congratulating team-mates shouldering me from the pitch. With absolutely no hesitation I kicked accurately into touch and the referee blew for no-side on a nil-nil draw. Both teams ignored me and I never played again. The spell was broken. But whether the game will ever be demystified enough in Wales for those who wish so to be able to ignore it altogether is more than doubtful. We pass the obsession on to our children, almost un- wittingly, like a fear of the dark. Anyone for snooker?

On the Pill

History, taste or fashion can conceal a writer from us. We inherit a prejudice, and unless something impels us to explore that writer's work with an open mind and gauge for ourselves his or her real achievement, we will believe in the lie forever. We think in slogans and headlines, and whether aware of it or not, the mind will tie its labels, second-hand, borrowed yet unquestioned images, that as slowly and irrevocably as silt create the sediment of popular mythology.

So the poems of William Henry Davies are facile and lyrical: child-like, spontaneous, unpolitical and supremely uncerebral. Even people who have never read a poem in their lives know what a Nature Poet is, and somehow over the years we have been able to dismiss Davies with that hugely vague yet damning epitaph. In short we have sanitized him. Our literary critics have somehow allowed to take place an act of cosmetic surgery that now obscures from view the real Davies, the alcohol-addicted, sexually-ravenous traveller, oddjobber and vagrant. Thus his work lies almost unreachably behind the 'genteel' façade of so-called Georgian poetry. God knows how many other fine and original writers are imprisoned under that now seemingly immovable slab. I'm not making a case for W.H. Davies as the Rimbaud of Portland Street, Pillgwenlly, but it appears to me indisputable that he wrote of aspects of life that few subsequent Welsh poets have ventured into, either from choice, experience or scruples. Poverty, crime, homelessness, defiantly unromantic back-lane sex, boredom and despair were his best subjects. Today we can trendily bracket it all together as 'low-life', but 'real life' is its best description. For me, W.H. Davies is the first important English-language Welsh writer, and for all his treacly love verse, his ironic nostalgia for green Llantarnam and Llanwern, and even his sometimes incredible adoption of exhausted clichés and mannerisms, he possessed a technical skill and above all an imagistic power that few more modern Welsh writers have ever matched.

Examining photographs and paintings of the poet does something to clear the Georgian mist. He was a little bull of a man with the tanned, hard-bargaining expression of an outdoor market trader. The famous portraits by Knight and John perhaps exaggerate the essential sensuality of the face, but the thick coxcomb of dark hair, always luxuriantly coiffured, is genuine enough. For as fame attached itself to him, a suggestion of dandyism became more apparent. But it is the eyes that strike you most forcibly. They are large, deep, dark-lashed and strongly feminine. Davies himself boasted that he had the ability to look harder and longer, to discover more in the visible, than most other men. Indeed some of his poems seem to describe trance-like conditions brought on by unflinching bouts of acute, unblinking observation. Nobody looked as William Davies did.

And perhaps if we made the effort to re-read his poetry, we might be brought to think a little about the Pillgwenlly dockland, the area that bred W.H. Davies. I don't think the writer had any particular love for the place, and he left its confines soon enough, but it made an impression on his writing. Walking around you can see why, but unfortunately now there is no-one to celebrate or mourn over an area that still demands its own poet. Pass down Commercial Street towards the docks and look behind a planked-up window not far from the narrow, moss-coloured frontage of the Falcon Hotel. Usually inside are an old man and a very old woman laboriously tying up bundles of newly cut firewood. Their overcoats are tied together with the same hairy string that binds the sticks. Behind them, through a side entrance, are stacked window-frames, doorjambs and varnished banisters filched from the overflowing skips and derelict terrace houses of Pillgwenlly. Such workers, and their ramshackle squats, were typical subjects for the unsentimental compassion of Davies's poetry. If we could look, as he looked, we might discover far more than we ever thought existed in our cities and towns.

I passed the Italo-Welsh Club and the Irish Club, the seamen's outfitters and the spice-filled Indian grocery markets. At lunch-time going into the Tredegar and the West of England I shared the curious guilty torpor of the afternoon drinkers. Having nowhere better to go and nothing better to do might have been scrawled on placards and hung round the necks of these few customers. Gentle, unwitting subversives, they watched the pool balls scatter on the baize and the veins of foam run down their glasses. Conversation was precious for its rarity. I was disappointed. A tourist seeking local colour, I had somehow imagined such places would be like that long-lamented Wild West saloon, the Mount Stuart Hotel in Cardiff's dockland, where one Friday afternoon I opened a magazine with a picture of a boxer on the front and found myself surrounded by a bar full of ex-champions and young contenders. But here on the Pill I had only discovered a worrying absence of people. Further down the road an old Plaid Cymru office was an empty billet, the floor strewn with newspapers and junk mail, an emphatic 'AR GAU' taped to the glass. It was towards afternoon closing that I entered the Waterloo.

This is an immense redbrick Victorian hotel with a tower that serves as a landmark for ships returning to Newport. Inside, a few drinkers were lost in the gloom, hunched round an incongruously modern fruit-machine. Wooden drinking-stalls, a long, ornately-tiled bar, original brass lamp-fittings and three-legged pub tables could not fill its overpowering emptiness. Time, like trade, had stopped. There were no ships now, and the lunchtime executive set had not yet been able to turn it into a lasagne-and-lager re- creational facility. Stained-glass reflected a brilliant quilt of colours across the smoke-room: bronze-painted pillars like Victorian street- lights supported the highest ceiling I had ever seen in a pub. When I sipped, I sipped reverentially, savouring the almost cathedral-like calm, until the other drinkers left and the landlady immediately won £8.20 of their money on the machine they had been stubbornly feeding.

So what happens to a frontier town when they move the frontier? In the case of Newport it remains doggedly and unapologetically itself, its manifestations of cultural schizophrenia remarkably few. And if signs of cultural anything seem rather scarce there today, that cannot be honestly applied to its dockland area. Working class, run down, quieter than it should be, but still impressive, Pillgwenlly retains echoes of that big bang of cosmopolitanism that transformed Welsh seaports in the last century. Directions for Dociau Casnewydd might be written in Urdu or Mandarin or

Gujarati. Yet more important is the fact that the people know each other and extend greetings on the street; and if they cannot afford to drink in the afternoon, they maintain an inner-city community that, miraculously, the developers haven't ripped to pieces.

I walked round the unremarkable terraces where William Davies was brought up, down Frederick Street and into King's Parade. In my mind were the words of another Welsh poet, a recent pronouncement to the effect that most South Walians were ignorant of their history and guilty of corrupting their own language. Nothing unusual about that, I suppose. In any tribe the role of remembrancer is a specialized job. Over half a pint of acrid coffee in a Pill cafe I listened to a world news bulletin entirely full of the exploits of the cast of our British soap-opera. And Both and Fergie and Sir Bob turned the corner with me and stepped past Bolt Street School. It was true. The people I spoke to were concerned with the present, with perhaps half an eye on the future. This was Newport, and up the road lay John Frost Square. But here the Chartists were a group of contemporary folk musicians, play-ing that evening in the town centre. A line of their posters twitched on a zinc wall. And Supertramp, of course, was only a name on the Tredegar jukebox, a collection of rock stars exiled from their mansions.

Despairing protestations about a people's cultural amnesia are as futile as William Davies's hankerings after green Llanwern. And a lot less memorable. Today the struggle in Pillgwenlly is to keep bricks and mortar together and the population decently housed. Already too many of the windows are shattered and too many front doors lead only to noxious barracks for rats and perhaps the occasional non-supertramp. The dockland needs a poet with both eyes on the present and the brilliant immediacy of image-making once shown by W.H. Davies. For there is, I imagine, a development plan for Pillgwenlly, as there is for every other port and resort in the country. A barrage across the Usk to hide away that superb but tourist-daunting expanse of olive mud, a marina, a theme-park devoted to some municipal concept of leisure, all of these probably exist right now as part of a blueprint for Newport's future prosperity. And whether we should wish to preserve the ancient, decaying pilings around the transporter bridge, the grimy corbels and architraves of Commercial Street, or that extraordinary Victorian drinking-museum of the Waterloo are debatable points. But what is certain is that if we create an area in Pillgwenlly where people cannot live where they work or work where they live, we will be diminishing this still vital corner of Newport, to the detriment of the town and to Wales. And in the process damaging all of our cultures. Embarrassed by the uncomfortable power and startling language of Pill's William Davies, we have managed through apologetic biography and critical ineptitude to castrate the poet. I would hate to see these few working-class streets and their muted but unselfconscious celebration of the dangerous here-and-now hosed down as clean and quiet as everywhere else.

Positively Fink Street

Monday

Virgin Atlantic is the Fun Airline. To prove it they make you watch a series of video nasties throughout the flight. In these short films various rock groups mime to their best records. They start doing this even before the stewardesses have finished their own mime about what happens when the aircraft plunges into the sea. I think I liked The Damned best, a jolly set of boys wandering about in graveyard mist. What they were singing about, however, I could not tell you, as I was too old-country to shell out the six dollars for use of headphones.

'Why do you wish to enter the United States?'

After an hour's logjam at passport control the queue is moving.

And boy, have we shown them how to queue.

'Er, to read poetry.'

The immigration official gives me a pitying look, but soon I am out in the cool Jersey air, breathing lead-free exhaust and feeling all the better for it. And an hour later hurtling towards the Bronx in a yellow-cab. Jetlag is no match for adrenalin, and I congratulate myself on feeling so sharp. However, perhaps I was a little slow when I let the hoodlum on Eighth Avenue relieve me of ten dollars in a definitely one-sided transaction. And is that the time or the taxi fare in glowing green numbers on the dash? The cab decelerates and stops.

The driver slowly turns round.

'Hey man, you must know this area a whole lot better than me.'

'No chance. Why?'

'Coz we're lost, man.'

'Lost?'

'Yeah, lost.'

Tuesday

New York's got plenty but it hasn't got what New London's got. New London's got nuclear submarines. There's one now, a skeletal gleam in its marine hangar, a corset of scaffolding crawling with spidery platelayers. Amtrak cuts through the Fall and here's Boston, sane city of banks and galleries and a hundred thousand students. Ninety-seven have turned up tonight to the Public Library, to hear about Gaelic survivals in Cape Breton. First night of the Interkelt International Conference and guess who's on tomorrow night exactly at this time. I take my luggage into the lecture hall and slump in the darkened aisle. Immediately a man is standing in front of me writhing in elaborate mime. He is a young man with an angry moustache. 'I shouldn't sit here?' He cocks his head like a furious budgerigar. 'I shouldn't put my bags there?' With beautiful disdain he shows he can only understand the Gaels of Cape Breton with at least three empty seats on either side of him. Sane city. Cool city.

Wednesday

On stage with me are two grand pianos and an American flag. Poetry has shrivelled up and died in too many places like this, but at least the mike is less the alien truncheon it might have been, and it's easier not to shout. But if you get too close to the silver golfball there's a strange popping sound, like peapods bursting under your thumb. I think I shelled a lot of peas tonight.

Thursday

In search of the chic bistros and preppy pubs of Boston's Quincy Market, I end up in the definitely unfashionable suburb of Quincy. Feeling a pang, I decide to enter a pizza hut. Feeling another pang I order a 'large' pizza. At home these are decent sized and cheaply priced. Over here I am very soon to be proved a novice in the arcane art of pizza-ordering. Five minutes later a waiter staggers to the counter with a waggonwheel-sized disk of piebald pastry covered with enough mozzarella to immediately gum up all my major arteries. This is a mistake. This is not a mistake? The waiter calls me back as I tiptoe to the exit, and I am forced to take the UFO shaped Italian manhole cover to a table. Jesus. Do I look like a coach-party? This thing is four feet across. The rest of the café is deserted except for a gang of pizza-faced thugettes spreadeagled over the video-games, and a swarthy washer-up, twitching a towel and eyeing me from the wings. I give him a smile which is supposed to mean 'Wow!' but he turns to his grey pillar of chilli bowls and the girls get on with beating each other up. Across the table the vast pie sits bubbling, but I am already halfway down the street.

Friday

Sense of direction is not a strong suit, but tonight my mental compasses are haywire. First left, straight on, first left, and I should have been at the back door of Joe and Gerrie Clancy. Instead here is the Bronx night closing in, black as an abandoned warehouse. Unfamiliar corners lead to the blind backs of garages and alsatians erect behind wiremesh. A line of rubbish skips are pale lozenges in the weak street-light, while beside a mechanic's shed gas-bottles hang like chrysalids. But above my head looms the first clue for a long time. A green New York plate says Fink St. Never heard of it, but I think we deserve each other. Towards White Plains a police siren trails its bubbles of sound. An alsatian drags its chain across the lot.

Saturday

Registration plates in New Hampshire carry the state motto 'Live Free or Die'. The car park's full of this philosophy, but soon we're in thick woodland, and eventually find ourselves on top of Mystery Hill. From a mile away comes the sound of muskets. They're replaying the Revolutionary War up here, in between the barbecues, and there are occasional glimpses of tattered redcoats fleeing through the trees. But for someone like me without a proper concept of American history, there's a bigger surprise coming. Mystery Hill, awful Disney name it might be, is the site of the American Stonehenge. Suddenly, in a clearing of the trees there are standing stones and burial chambers, in fact all the mute and puzzling Neolithic clutter normally associated with Carnac or Callanish. Originally written off by British archaeologists as a recent folly, the stones of Mystery Hill are now believed to have been put in place by Celtic voyagers, long before any supposed 'Welsh' or 'Viking' discovery of America. Hundreds of less spectacular but equally ancient sites have been discovered across the country. An extensive ogham script was recently found in a cave in West Virginia. At dusk on this hilltop, amongst the boulders and red maples, I'm prepared to believe anything, and chew thoughtfully on a chocolate-coated peanut butter bar, kindly provided by the American Stonehenge shop and information centre. There's intermittent musket fire in the valley as the live free or die society gets an action replay of its formation. Up here I sit on a slab once used apparently as a sacrificial altar. There's an elaborate stone gutter for collecting blood. Strange, I thought us Celts were supposed to be the good guys.

Sunday

I'm reliably informed that in the childhood of our more distant ancestors, Roy Rogers was a hero of the American West. It now appears the same RR has given up hustling rustlers and is busy cornering part of the vast US junkfood market, in the form of Roy Rogers Drive-In Breakfast Bars. New Jersey is full of them. Or is it Delaware? I'd like to drive in and sample a brontoburger, but I don't think Roy grills those yet. He's more liable to wreck your day with a hot hero or a cold sub. Anyway, Trailways aren't stopping for breakfast, and Roy's yellow ranch vanishes behind the peepshow hoardings and electric graffiti advertizing 'live girls'. Which I suppose is a relief. And it's definitely Delaware. In New Jersey you can't smoke on the bus or take liquor outside a bar. And sex is either bluecollar or subversive. Perhaps that's why the state song is Springsteen's 'Born to Run'. Trigger, by the way, is in California. Stuffed.

Monday

In Washington the students are laid back. Literally. There are no chairs in this room, only a series of carpeted tiers on which thirty literature majors loll, squat, crouch, lounge. And lie. A boy and girl wrapped around each other like loving boa-constrictors gently pop potato crisps into each other's mouths. Someone else has placed several pizza slices on the floor like pieces from a huge jigsaw. After the first poem one third of the audience gets up and leaves. By half way another ten have gone, but a different ten have taken their places, while outside in the corridor the electric whinny of video games and coke dispensers give the words a nervous reggae backbeat. I think fondly of the young man in Boston Public Library and his determined concentration. But even he had a styrofoam vase of pink and yellow popcorn wedged between his thighs. During the last poem another sizeable chunk of the audience quits. Was it anything I said? Anyway it's over, and of course it is very difficult to applaud from a prone position. As I ask for questions the one o' clock buzzer goes and the lit. buffs scatter for burgers and shakes. But there's still one student, a pale, ascetic-looking youth, probably something of a budding poet himself, keen for a few tips. He picks up his papers and comes over.

'Can I help?' I ask brightly.

'Yeah. I bought too much pizza in refectory. Wanna slice?'

Tuesday

On a train to New York a Brazilian composer buys me seven bottles of beer. Between drinks he shows off the Tibetan grammar he's studying and offers to introduce me to Leonard Bernstein. Already stoned, he visits the toilet every quarter hour for a suck of his Green Mountain reefer. I can't buy my own booze because my wallet's been stolen but that particular tragedy is starting to wane. The composer is a people collector, as gay as a lark, and excellent company. Soon he has our whole compartment talking – the German student, the New England teacher, the insurance rep and the blonde with neon lipstick. He made his money by writing the music for a horror flick, the type where lots of people get chopped into lots of pieces. He saw the cheque but never the film, and is now living in style off the proceeds. Another Moulsons arrives. Then a Heineken. Then Grand Metropolitan Station where we are bundled out and stare unsteadily at a blur of escalators. Arriving drunk in New York is perhaps the best way to greet the city. And the thought that your money has already been stolen is strangely comforting.

Wednesday

Flying home I watch a very orthodox Jewish pair presented with special foil and plastic wrapped kosher Virgin dinners. They hold up these icy rectangles of mid-flight microwave technology to the red dawn light, but it seems the tablets pass muster, as gently their seals are broken and the pale meats and cuboid veg lifted into the gentlemen's beards. Across the plane, someone in Middle Eastern robes has strapped a contraption to his chest and is down on his knees in prayer. It doesn't look like a parachute but perhaps he knows something we don't. But the Fun Airline plunges on and soon the video is hissing again. What's more, the gentlemen of The Damned are with us in person, admiring their screen images. A troupe of punkish undertakers, they watch themselves strumming amidst the foggy crypts. And it pays to have a rock group on board. At customs, while a mêlée of blueshirted officials loot the cases of these obvious dopefiends, the rest of our party walk through unnoticed.

Taking It

In any league table of the world's most inhospitable places, the waiting rooms at Department of Health and Social Security offices must feature near the top. Though notices on every wall forbid smoking, the carpet beneath your feet will be reduced to a kind of nylon coral-reef by the burning stubs trodden into the weave. Khaki and mushroom-painted walls hold a hundred curling messages stating in incomprehensible jargon the rights of claimants. Coloured posters, listing the dangers of drinking, eating, not exercising, making false claims and generally taking any diversion from the intolerably straight and narrow, entertain the patient queues waiting to be told their financial fate, either for the week or the rest of their lives. And behind a grubby green pane or a grille as fine as a chip-pan will sit an over-worked clerk preparing to honour your appointment, and totally oblivious of the terror caused by the most innocent glance in your direction.

I visited such an office recently in order to explain a small economic predicament. Slowly, I started conversations with the people ahead and behind me in the queue. The woman in front had brought two children into the waiting-room. They danced between the chairs, thin and cleanly dressed, language unintelligible and their pinched faces full of E numbers and videos. The mother smoked incessantly, but so did everyone in the room except myself and the two small boys. Shoes, she said, shoes and heating were the problems, and the way that clothes went damp, even in the wardrobes, because of all the condensation in the house. There was a bruise far up on her temple under her hair and a red bite-mark on the side of her neck. Her mouth shone with a line of startling orange lipstick, perfectly preserved despite the cigarettes. The children constantly demanded sweets and drinks, but I don't think I heard her speak a single word to them. It was the second time that week she had made the journey from her mountain-top council flat to the department. She came out from her appointment while I was still in the queue, a sea-green giro cheque rolled into a tube tight as a cigarette, the children exploding like fireworks about the strip-lit waiting room.

In spite of the spring warmth the man behind me kept on his massively stained overcoat. He had walked ten miles from his home valley to this office clutching clothes in one carrier bag and two plastic flagons of cider in another. He brandished a bottle now, swigging deeply and offering the liquor around as if he understood the frustration and nervousness of most of the people in the room, and would try to lift the atmosphere. There were no takers and the drinker continued happily to describe his last drying-out session in the local mental hospital, and the exhausting achievement of getting himself banned from all of the thirty-four public houses in this town. It is weeks now since the visit but I have not been able to forget this character. I think about his rank clothes, his alcoholism, his untanglable bush of beard and black hair. Above all I acknowledge his need to chronicle his own history and the skill with which he achieved this. Such a confrontational style of living, unapologetic, incorrigible, lonely, seemed to throw the rest of us in the room into pallid relief.

My interview passed as painlessly as I suppose these things possibly can. It was concerned totally with money: what I was owed, and what I earned. It would be foolish to be misled by false notions of camaraderie and shared experience while waiting in a queue in the DHSS, but I came out of the concrete high-rise at least a little warmer for feeling the sardonic humour and indomitable bloodymindedness of the other citizens under investigation. And there is no bureaucracy yet developed that can snuff out the power of the scrumpy-fuelled childhood reminiscences of a gentleman of the Mid Glamorgan roads, especially when the malodorous dregs of his flagon are being shaken over its green monitored word processor. Scenes like the latter might be valuable now only for their rarity. The economy, we are told, has picked up and market forces have created prosperity. The whole of South Wales is part of the London commuter-belt, while a sea of gentrification is lapping at the shores of Tonypandy and Brynaman. Dole queue drama is yesterday's hype, or so it would appear from the property supplements of our national newspapers.

Yet the descent in the juddering DHSS lift reminded me of a job

I had finished a few weeks previously. The description had seemed straightforward enough. Take a class of adults for a morning's creative writing course. I arrived at an estate, every street of which was named after the illustrious dead of English literature, and after abandoning the car in a maze of eighteenth-century Romantics, eventually found the address, a link-house used by a variety of residents and charity groups as a meeting place.

Amazingly, thirteen people had turned up for the experiment. Unsurprisingly twelve of these were women, three of whom had come equipped for a calligraphy class. (Despite a few heroic ambassadors for the cause, the term 'creative writing' remains meaningless for most people.) The class met for seven consecutive Wednesday mornings, its numbers varying between five and eighteen. During the whole period not one single word was written. There was no time for it, as the group's energy was devoted to bitter, yet comic descriptions of life on the estate. Eighty per cent of the adult population was unemployed: having an address 'up in the poets on top of the mountain' was an inevitable local stigma that started in nursery school, led to violence and feuding in the comprehensive, and generated the antipathy of every political party. The children sniffed glue and break-danced in the filthy play-areas provided – windswept concrete yards and bunkers filled with refuse. Most mothers remained like agoraphobics within the home, confined by lack of money and the intense male chauv-inism – one of the most irreducible of all Welsh characteristics – to lives of washing, tranquilliser addiction and TV. And the men? The men seemed to spend a lot of time in small groups around cars jacked up on breeze-blocks or lighting fires in back-yards. We would see them as the class abandoned its shabby front room and marched out on expeditions around the estate.

The women took me to the flats where many of them lived. These were five-storey redbrick high-rises with broken lifts, hallways littered with syringes, excrement and glue-bags, and more graffiti than New York subway trains. The architect responsible for these buildings had been awarded a gold medal. Curiously his designs had omitted drying areas for wet clothes, so that the only places to hang a wash were window ledges. Another small difficulty created by his triumphant blueprint was that the estate roads were too narrow to give access to refuse lorries. To solve this problem concrete compounds had been built on the peripheries of the estate, where the residents were supposed to deposit their black rubbish-bags. Dogs rooted through these dumps and children kicked open the sacks. The result was that the whole area looked like a Cardiff street after an International. Takeaway dinners and disposable nappies spread across the open-plan, while in their play-bunkers the children built bonfires of old mattresses and cardboard. Another problem was tipping. Rubbish attracts rubbish, and building contractors and residents of other districts would travel to the estate and unload their own waste.

Back at the meeting house we talked of demonstrations, petitions and political poetry. Letters to the press and local councillors were discussed, and clean-up campaigns devised. I did nothing during these visits but listen and remember, learning especially about the energies that poverty destroys, and the vitality and humour that are debilitated by having to exist on giro-money. I also confronted the nature of a system that takes care of its sick, its unemployed, its depressed, its incapable and its fearful with derisory handouts that can only ensure a lifestyle characterized by meanness and inactivity. Early on in our meetings I asked a blunt question: 'Why don't you do something about all this?' The replies were defensive but grew in spirit. Poverty shrinks self-confidence. Like a disease it takes away physical strength and numbs the imagination. The middle-aged grandmothers in the room, their daughters in obligatory stone-washed denim the colour of cigarette smoke, and Ashley, the one man in the group, gleaming with a splendid sense of indignation rekindled after a lost decade of tranquillized introspection, laughed at my naivety.

Doing something was coming to class, was talking together about the common problems. For some, attendance in this scruffy room was a victory. It was a triumph over that fretful lethargy with which our social security system infects so many people.

'Why do you take it?' I goaded.

'Because we've always taken it,' shouted Ashley. 'And remember. You're the only person paid to be here. There's a thousand people on this estate all locked up with their junk food and their junk videos and their tablets. The kids rebel by drinking or smashing windows, but that's only hurting themselves. No one's doing anything because everybody's frightened. If you can't say either yes or no to every question the DHSS asks, they'll brand you as a trouble-maker or a problem case and your money will stop. Anything uncertain in between, which after all applies to most of us, is impossible for them to understand. They haven't got a little box for reality on those forms of theirs. It's just like it's been all through history. That Crawshay Bailey who lived up the valley in Aber-aman in his big house with fish-ponds and ornamental trees – do you know what he used to pay his workers with? Tokens. Tokens like cloakroom tickets or snakes-and-ladders counters. You could only spend the tokens in his shops on goods he supplied. Otherwise you'd starve. That's a pretty sharp system and as far as I'm concerned the giro is just the same.'

I came out of the lift and crossed the car-park. Ahead of me were the woman and her two hyperactive sons, the boys leaping star- shaped against the bright noon. She lit another cigarette and teetered along in red high heels towards the bus station and Lewistown. Behind me the cider-drinker was blinking at the light, suddenly uncertain. One day, I thought, somebody is going to invent socialism. But even then people like this will have to go on taking it.

Animal Crackers

The wine was fine and the beer the tipple of a connoisseur. Deliberately clouded with a potent yeast, small slices of lemon had been placed at the bottom of each glass, and now effervesced ferociously. The brew, admittedly, did look like murky aquarium water, and this regional speciality had not totally convinced me of the need for another round, but, as I said to the others at the table, I was prepared to try anything. Except the meat. Any meat. This had been off my personal menu for nearly twenty years, and I was not going to lapse now, especially while the veal, pale and delicate as young violets, was being handed around by the waiter.

I was not the only one with such stern principles in this Bavarian restaurant. Others had brought the same determination into the heart of the meat-eating world, and perhaps were starting, very slightly, to regret it. I looked at my friend opposite and his first victuals that day. His bowl contained a thin cirrus of lettuce, bathed in a vinegar dressing sharper, he said, than the solvents he remembered using in O Level chemistry experiments. There were pieces of tomato, no bigger than nail-pairings, swimming around with an onion slice, curved and gleaming like a sickle, in the acid rain of his German salad. I possessed a similar bowl, but also cheese and eggs and the undoubtedly fortifying beer. My companion opposite, a confirmed vegan and teetotaller, the purest of the pure and abstemious to what I considered a dangerous degree, could not find satisfaction here. I watched him snatch the green transparent star at the centre of a cucumber slice as if it was a phial of vitamin pills. And a baby never seized a nipple with greater need than this lean, bestubbled botanist as he pierced the crimson globe of a radish and released its primitive flavour. Beside his plate a glass of mineral water was slowly calming down. Like the vegetables, I knew this tasted of subterranean darkness, of a philosophy that admitted no artificial stimulants, of that cool and slightly bitter regime of health of which I too was a convinced yet hopelessly errant disciple.

Maybe that is not strictly true. I did not become a vegetarian be- cause of a wish to turn my body into a temple of cleanliness and inoffensive odours, and my subscription to *Health and Beauty* was renewed for far more fundamental reasons than a belief in the efficiency of diet or exercise. I became a vegetarian because my whole family did. When I was a teenager a slaughterhouse was built at the edge of the village where we lived. This replaced the blood-soaked shambles of immemorial memory, the original stonework and convoluted yards of which had made it look like an unrestored medieval inn. We watched the herds and flocks ushered towards the killing-floors with promises, deceit and brutality. We noted how electric prods helped in this process. At the same time the principles of battery farming were receiving much television publicity, my mother, particularly impressing me with imagery of rural Wales as a vast concentration camp for animals. So one evening the four of us renounced the chop, the steak, the rasher and the burger. After some debate, fish was included in the boycott, along with battery-farmed eggs. As none of us in the household possessed much culinary imagination, this immediately created problems, and for the next ten years our diet consisted largely of tinned soup, crisps, and Mother's Pride, all inevitably concocted with a huge variety of animal-derived substances. However, as our decision had been an emotional one, research into such matters was usually very sketchy: there was also the distinct feeling, usually at mealtimes, that we were doing more than our bit. (For those who are interested, nearly twenty years later only two of the original four who took the great oath against meat still tread the path of virtue. The others have gone back to scoffing sausages created from minced bowel and sawdust, and those dinosaur-spined pasties which seem to contain traces of every vital bodily organ.)

People who learn that I am a vegetarian ask if I have always hated meat. I reply that I have never disliked the taste, smell or anything else of frying bacon or spluttering roast. Unlike other vegetarians, over-fastidious people probably, to whom the sight of a great marbled salami or the whiff of a charring steak can be the causes of physical sickness, I can appreciate the value and the quality of meat. But after twenty years of almost total renunciation it is the easiest thing in the world to sit bathed in hickory chip woodsmoke and feel no temptation to join in the feast as conglomerates of shredded foreskin and ragged eyelid are shared round the happy throng. No, I have never hated meat, and a recent experience has taught me more of its value.

I was minding a bookshop for a friend, and between customers was flicking through a glossy paperback entitled *The SAS Guide to Survival*. Thus I now know the way to behave when confronted by a Komodo Dragon, and how to survive after parachuting without compass or provisions on to an Antarctic island. In theory I have learned how to make a life-raft from a pair of trousers, and the best way to disperse a chanting mob of dangerous rioters. What were most interesting, however, were the passages devoted to the insides of animals. The first thing a desperate SAS member learns is not to waste any part of the beast that conveniently drops dead in front of him. Blood makes a succulent pudding, and the juices of the stomach serve as a useful acid. Intestinal casing, having been thoroughly washed and scoured, can be employed as wrapping paper for sending presents home, whilst the marrow bones of this much reduced creature should be cracked and sucked like yellow sherbet-bombs, for the life-enhancing crystal jelly they luckily contain. Only the liver poses a problem. The SAS author, veteran of forty years of conflict and global tight corners, had never been able to come to terms with liver. In his view, the liver was an aggregate of poisons, the dustbin of the body. Parasites and bodily intruders apparently home in on this organ, a real mecca for undesirables. Don't eat the livers of monkeys or elephants, warned the military scribe. Indeed, tropical livers should always be avoided, whilst those from temperate zones must be examined prior to consumption. Passing butcher-shops these days I therefore look carefully at the unblemished burgundy satin from which Welsh liver is composed. Little that's dangerous there it seems.

Vegetarianism poses its worst problems for those who attend conferences or visit restaurants of a typical standard. Jellified cheese sauces and rubber omelettes are the usual alternatives provided for these difficult customers. Some of the most wretched meals I have ever consumed have been served at university buffets, places where I would have thought the non-meat philosophy had long been embraced. Fast-food, likewise, is not designed with the vegetarian in mind. I remember reaching a low point of hunger one night in Buffalo, when, waiting for a coach, I was compelled in my light-headed state to enter a MacDonald's Hamburger Bar. Over a carton of animal fat-dunked 'fries', really pipecleaners erect in a rigor mortis of batter, and a huge polystyrene vessel, the size of a grave-vase, filled with enough Coke, I was convinced, to dissolve my fillings, I watched America's burger mountain slowly expand. As I loitered in this neon shed, I calculated that Mac-Donald's in that time had levelled fifty more acres of Panamanian rainforest for the grazing of their hamburger cattle. A few days later I gained revenge by purchasing *The Jungle* by Upton Sinclair, one of the most powerful descriptions of capital's exploitation of the working class and man's vileness to the animal kingdom ever written. Outside my window the spits and griddles of New York were being loaded for a long night's feasting, but I was in Chicago, ankle-deep in the bodily fluids of the stockyards, remembering the unearthly cries from the abattoir in my village in Wales, the vixen-like wailings of an imprisoned herd waiting for the morning's knife.

George Orwell detested vegetarians. Such people believed in pixies, he claimed, and all the trappings of an effete, middle-class, 'alternative' culture. Veggies wore straggling beards, sandals and unravelling jerseys. Their timorous hearts pumped the body's equivalent of alcohol-free lager around their trembling extremities. I remembered this the first time I met my wife's parents, wincing at the incomprehension in their Yorkshire eyes when it was announced I would not be helping dismantle the Sunday roast. The Pennine breeze that whipped up the snickets and down the ginnels behind the house was a soothing balm compared with their expressions.

Ten years later that image problem remains in place. Recently I have been teaching in a primary school named after a murderer and kidnapper. The school is located on a slope above the country's greatest industrial anachronism, a factory producing smokeless fuel, and creating in the process, a huge quantity of flame and poisonous fumes which it pours into the already muggy atmosphere through a phalanx of forty-five chimneys. In the staffroom, this plant is known as Dante's Inferno, a hopeful poetic glimmer in a culture of kazoos and videos. I had come to the school to encourage the writing of poetry, and had announced for the cooks' benefit my reluctance to eat meat. As I had already disappointed the staff by not arriving dressed in a tam-o'-shanter and long black overcoat, clutching a human skull as an aid to creative writing, this at least served as a suitable eccentricity.

Yet, there is a basic sanity in vegetarianism which I find increasingly important. Meat-eating appears to me now a manic, almost hysterically self-deluding activity, the carnivores amongst us clinging to an out-dated habit with obtuse deliberation. For we all know about the evils of battery-farms and intensive meat production – not that knowing about these crimes will achieve much. Ever since Biafra we have looked at our television screens and watched people starve to death, and in twenty years not taken effective action against world hunger. So what chance is there of subverting the Christmas Dinner industry? The truths of unnecessary cruelty to, and the almost inconceivable exploitation of, domesticated animals are only other additions to that strange dark area at the back of the mind where we accumulate the guilt for actions we know will never cease.

Breath of the Dragon

They had made their camp in the sand above the high-tide margin and now stared down the wide beach out to sea. Both were fashionably remote behind the black slash of sunglasses that divided their faces, content to be defined by the music from their cassette-player, the dark prow of their powerboat lying behind them, pointing at the sky from a smashed dune. Beside cooled their dainty Japanese beachmobile, parked in a bed of sea-holly, and next to that a corral of bottles, clothes and barbecue equipment had been arranged. Here was summer's expeditionary force in virgin holiday territory. To the rear, a mile down the coast, the infantry were already digging in for the season's occupation.

I nodded and didn't wait for any response, feeling my determination to inform this couple that they were breaking the law turn to a foolish officiousness. Their dune-flattening, orchid-obliterating progress through this site of special scientific interest was still vivid in my mind. I had followed their blue trail of diesel over the summits to this isolated bay, intent on a reasonable explanation of how they were fouling up the whole works, not only for *Gymnadenia Conopsea*, but sensitive souls such as myself. Yet righteousness evaporated as I descended to the beach. Even these explorers, now busy constructing their idea of civilization out of reggae and sun-oil and blameless red wine, and blessed with an ability to penetrate the most obscure corner of the reserve, had not been able to travel beyond the tidal reach of twentieth-century pollution. In the sand about their camp lay the plastic tubs and rusted aerosols that they were innocent of dropping. On the beach in front of them gleamed the orange bread-trays and traffic-bollards these two adventurers had had no part in depositing. And amidst the flowers of the sea-rocket, its petals all the colours of Italian ice-cream, were scattered the bricks of yellow foam more usually associated with modern furniture making. The trespassers I had tracked down were stretched out amongst this rubbish, their bodies concentrating on the unspectacular sunshine. I wondered if they even noticed the destruction around them, or like most of us, were merely resigned to it as a regrettable but inescapable part of life.

It is one of the more blatant contemporary hypocrisies that we are able to dislike tourism and tourists while frequently indulging with relish our own desires to travel out of our locales and squat, however damagingly, elsewhere – Venice or Llangrannog, Bala or Biarritz, it doesn't really matter on the place. The tourist is despised, and has become a figure of fun in modern folklore, precisely because all of us know exactly what it is like to be one of these wretched creatures. Tourists are destructive, ignorant, arrogant and immensely pathetic, and we only fool ourselves if we don't understand how they feel. For the tourist is the prime example of the passive, non-contributing, hungry-eyed, empty-headed victim that our culture would have us all become. I feel it myself every time I put a new film in the camera, buy the tickets or the map, and fill a suitcase with hideous but obligatory leisure-wear. The end of the journey is always a place where you can add nothing, offer nothing, only take from; a place you will drift through without comprehension or love. I look down the streets of my own town and see such visitors, and mingling with the scorn, that most rapid of all emotions, is, I hope, at least a little sympathy. The tourist bears the marks of his caste with as much dignity as he can muster. He acknowledges that his fate of a day, a fortnight, a year, God help him, is to accept society's plan to turn him into a spectator, never a participator, a human sponge. He understands that holidays are like temporary lobotomies. What he might not be aware of is the trail of damage he leaves in the slow, aimless wake of his progress.

On the Algarve they are painting out the English signs on bars and shops. In Venice, even the café proprietors are protesting about the infinite pedestrian hordes shuffling about the piazzas with as much animation as abattoir cattle away from the stun-gun. And in the taverns of Andalucia, the accents of Glamorgan and Yorkshire set the locals peering ever more bleakly into their wine. In Wales, however, we have the Wales Tourist Board, an organization which in its brief history has had more effect on the landscape of the countryside, the features of the towns and the livelihoods of the population, than World War Two. With more and more people possessing money and increased leisure time, the tourism marketeers in this country are striving their hardest to convert Wales into a tantalising yet practical holiday prospect for the Western hemisphere's mobile millions. And what lies in store for the rest of Wales can be glimpsed today in the resort where I live.

The whole reason for the continuing existence of this town is that it is able to attract visitors to its brief yet frenetic high season. In the concerted effort to triple the population of the area for this period, a whole series of environmental crimes and planning misdemeanours has been cunningly perpetrated. One of the most spectacular involved the construction of what is known as a 'hydroslide' on one of the slightly less ravaged stretches of our coastline. Whenever I see this wonder I am transported back to fourth-form biology periods. One of the exercises then was to crayon, in as many colours as possible, a page-length drawing of the human alimentary canal. By the time I had reached the lower regions of the large intestine, I was usually reduced to using the purples, blacks and browns in the pencil-set, the disdained and hardly blunted pieces no other lesson demanded. Thus it is now an occasion for some nostalgia to round the corner of the Farmhouse Fry Self-Service Cafeteria in our resort's funfair and be confronted by a vast, semi-translucent mock-up in sewage-sludge coloured plastic of the human bowel. Moving closer you are able to witness the very process of digestion inside the coils and tubes of this major tourist attraction and visitor-inspiring initiative, as a multi-hued current of chyme rumbles through the pulsating hydroslide to emerge as a dripping and momentarily dazed gaggle of children, whose indulgent parents had thoughtfully paid £1.50 to have the living daylights knocked out of their offspring.

Yet even monstrosities such as this, constructed in the name of tourism, lose their power to shock. It is hard to remember what the slide replaced, and so full of its praises are the local holiday brochures that I can only puzzle on why it was not built before. Caravans have the same amnesiac effect. Hidden in the tarmac undulations that most of the resorts dunes have become, is the biggest caravan site in Western Europe, a township with its own cinema, shops, pubs and leisure centre. (Another feature of my own loss of memory is that I cannot recall how the country spent its time before the flat-roofed, jerry-built, disinfectant-reeking leisure centre was invented.) What was temporary holiday accommodation is now permanent home for many people. For once caravans are in place they never go away, and in fact have a mysterious sex-life of their own, multiplying like neat white caterpillars all over the hospitable *morfa* of Wales. But people have to live somewhere, and such a residential site can engender a community spirit and identity far livelier than that of the host resort. If it is tempting on occasions to bemoan the loss of the habitat the caravans destroyed, and the hares and vipers and bracken-patterned nightjars that commercialism replaced, it is impossible to wish peoples' lives away, or the struggling tendrils of a community that they have tried to foster in an awkward soil. These caravans have gardens, measured out in white-limed pebbles, and each as tiny as a grave-plot. Moreover, the vans themselves boast names, the older vehicles being by turn 'Inglewood' or 'Swn y Mor', the newer additions chancing the absurd with 'Tara' or 'Sara' or 'Janice' or 'Jane'. (My research proves that ninety per cent of caravans, at least in South Wales, are christened in the feminine.)

The Wales Tourist Board is all in favour of free love between caravans. It is also enthusiastic about dragons and their heraldic and mythological significance for the country. (Dragon farms, it is rumoured, will be among the next big WTB projects.) However, the tourist executives have never grasped the fact, available in all good fairy tales, that a dragon only makes a country famous by laying it waste. A million walking-boots on Snowdon, the gentle bob of plastic lemonade bottles in the green water of Abereiddi, the sky above Conwy Castle a cauldron of photo-oxidants: these are not merely unfortunate side-effects of Wales's popularity in the world. They are a direct result of the Wales Tourist Board's refusal to accept any responsibility for the environmental and cultural damage created by tourism, and of its inability to lobby for legislative changes that would result in a diminution of such destruction. But if the price is paid next year, or the year after, there is no real worry. Tourism is the same as any industry run on the governing principle of maximizing this year's profits. It is like a bureaucratically-encouraged form of acid rain that poisons the vitals of the organism it is in existence to support. And it is interesting that in literal translation from its Welsh-language title, the WTB can be rendered the Wales Board of Welcome. Perhaps one day its executives will awake to the fact that in many parts there is nothing left of Wales to welcome us. Touristville, as in the place where I live, has taken its place. So, a word of advice to any prospective visitors. For some real local colour when you drive to this resort, call at the Rock and Fountain Hotel and pick your way through the extraordinary squalor of its gentlemen's privy, and read in faded felt-tip beneath the rusty cistern a maxim I now offer for inclusion in next year's WTB handbook: 'Shoot a tourist today. You know it makes sense.'

Chamber of Horrors

The journalist had what he thought were the makings of a story, and wanted help. It had been simmering for months, he said, but what he lacked were the right contacts and, above all, hard facts. There were, he claimed, accumulated suspic-ions that our resort on the Bristol Channel showed a higher incidence of leukaemia cases than the country as a whole, and that this cluster of cancers had so far escaped proper investigation and analysis.

I replied that in the ten years I had lived there I had only once before discussed this rumour. Ironically this had been on the previous day with a young man who stated, brazenly enough, that it was a leukaemia 'hot-spot'. Moreover, he knew how this higher incidence occurred. The disease was caused by the radioactive emissions from the nuclear power station at Hinkley Point, thirty-five miles away in Somerset. The seaspray was laced with plutonium and other radioactive substances. Common knowledge, he shrugged, and reminded me of the leak of eight tonnes of contaminated carbon dioxide in November, 1985, which had been blown towards the Welsh coast, before being turned south-west by the wind. I mentioned this to the journalist, who covered a page with shorthand. Two months later his article is either unwritten, unfabricated or spiked.

That 'leukaemia clusters' occur around plutonium-using power stations and research establishments is now widely known. The nuclear reprocessing plant at Sellafield and the weapons development centre at Aldermaston are examples of this. But there is no absolute proof that it is plutonium that causes these cancers. Indeed, it has been estimated that naturally occurring radon gas is more of a threat to human health than the combined emissions of UK nuclear power stations, and that such inescapable radio- active materials account for between two and ten per cent of all British cancers. Yet the link, if not the ultimate proof, is there, and together with the unsolvable problem of what to do with nuclear waste, and the safety records of these plants, constitute a major part of the anti-nuclear argument.

This argument is now concentrated on the proposals to build a Pressurized Water Reactor at Hinkley Point, objections to which must be lodged with Somerset County Council or West Somerset District Council by the end of this year. The plant will be known as Hinkley 'C' (there are already two functioning reactors at the site) and Walter Marshall, Chairman of the CEGB, has made it plain in interviews that he sees no reason why new nuclear stations could not, in time, use up most of the alphabet. But if the PWR does go ahead, it will be built at a period when the Hinkley 'A' reactor is due for decommissioning. This operation, extra-ordinarily expensive and dangerous, has not yet been completed on any other nuclear plant in the world. To carry it out next door to a PWR would seem an interesting experiment in our capacity for foolhardiness.

It was with thoughts like this that I recently took my daughter into the duneland east of the town, up to the summit known as Cog y Brain. At home, the sea is an insomniac murmur at the end of our street. If we listen, it is always there, but mostly we ignore it until a low, electrical whisper finds its way into the room and I look around to switch off a plug. But here the channel drummed impressively against a landscape that has hardly changed since the Bronze Age, when a Neolithic field-system had been inundated by the mobile sands. In a hollow the blue leaves of a buckthorn colony trembled like water, and above that a traffic bollard crowned the slope of Twmpath Tom Brython. Two boys on speedway bikes, their wheels as big as lifebelts, were cutting furrows into the beach, and beyond them the tide was depositing its usual selection from the bilges of passing ships and our own pumped-out effluent, returned with interest. But at least we could see that pollution. It's easy to get paranoid about the nuclear industry because its leaks are only scientifically traceable: and if Chernobyl and Three Mile Island were ominous eruptions, the consequences of which are not yet fully understood, there have been enough problems with British nuclear plants in recent years for me to condemn (if only to myself) all of our technology as erratic and dangerous. Nuclear power can contribute about fifteen per cent of our present energy requirements. It is important but not indispensable. Yet if PWRs are built at Sizewell in Suffolk, at Hinkley and Trawsfynydd and other existing sites, our reliance will become irreversible. We will be locked into nuclear nationhood almost to the extent that the French are now.

Moving west we left the caravan sites behind and entered the fairground. The arcades were loud as aviaries and lit by tubes of staccato neon. We fed the machines our silver, lost, and watched the faces of the screen-studying children, all set in examination-type seriousness. Outside, I paid for two places on the water-chute, and the car hauled us slowly up the polished rail. It was late in the season and the breeze was fresh in our hair. Dragging my eyes away from the approaching sky I noticed my knuckles were white on the bar, and that there were so few people below us it hardly seemed worth opening. They stood in groups in the aisles between rides and watched the infants in yellow plastic trains chug through sand and cactus. Behind us now were the snow-tipped Alps and a group of smiling weather-worn models in national costume. Amongst the pines at the edge of the fair were pumice-coloured dinosaurs poised about a tropical lagoon, and beyond those the irregular roofs and paint-blistered corbels of the resort. The car creaked up the track and suddenly we were at the summit of the chute. I felt my daughter brace herself for the descent, and pressed my own feet into the darkness as if searching for a brake. Yet for one instant we did not move. We stayed stiff and breathless at the highest point of the town, and as I looked outwards I saw the long ranks of caravans reduced to a box of pastel colours, and behind those the contours of the dunes stretching to the sea. A confusion of hillocks stood above the buckthorn before merging with the beach. The tide was high and racing, but beyond that the water was the colour of the dark tyrannosaurus in the pine grove. In Somerset, the field-patterns were etched clearly on the cliffs, but the cobalt sky above looked near to combustion. I thought of the geography of south-west England and the great indentation around Watchet where the PWR may be built. From the rail in the sky it seemed possible to touch that coast; all distance vanished with this new dimension of sight.

My daughter's eyes stared straight down the track to the pond of oily water. Still the car did not move. Some teenage girls emerged from the Haunted House, laughing at the memory of skeletons, the red-eyed corpses that refused to lie down, while into the waxworks of torturers and celebrated psychopaths stepped the end-of-holiday couples. They came to look at the things we are capable of doing to one another, and all the banal instrumentation of pain. I stared at the opposite coast from a town where a few centimetres of sand separate the bones of a neolithic aristocracy from this summer's indestructible plastics. There was a real storm fermenting over there and diagonals of light flickered over the sky. Already we are the hostages of modern technology, yet if PWRs are built at Hinkley Point and the other favoured sites, most of us will never understand how much more dangerous the world has become. We don't seem able to make the connection any more between the quality of our lives and the health of our part of the planet. We are sealed with our comforts into nuclear bunkers of the senses and have only the feeblest notion of responsibility towards what is outside our immediate satisfaction. And most people have anyway given up all pretension of influencing how their environment is shaped around them. That is being taken care of by those who know best. If Hinkley 'C' goes ahead it will be founded primarily on public apathy, incomprehension and a blind faith in scientific progress. It will play no bigger part in our daily consciousness than the Bronze Age relics and plastic bottles of tanning cream lying together in the sand at the edge of town.

Perhaps that is what I like about the dunes – their invisible movements that trap items from all our cultures and preserve them as a record of our concerns and values. Like glaciers, they are data banks of what we thought lost, or wished to lose. What will be engulfed and recorded of the nuclear park Wales is becoming is anybody's guess, but the images this town has chosen to display from the past are the terrors of the equatorial swamp and the torture chamber, an accurate calculation that one of the public's greatest appetites is for the vicarious thrill of fear and disgust.

Of course there are exceptions. These days the phone goes frequently in the environmental information centre where I work, bringing calls from concerned families in England. Most of these people are considering buying a house in Wales (usually the Gwynedd area or north Powys) but first wish to check on Welsh radiation levels. They have heard about the caesium-carrying north Wales sheep and the Chernobyl-flavoured grass in the Snowdonia National Park. Their questions are apologetic and simple. Is living in Wales safe, and what are the main radiation-free areas of the country? One lady wanted to know if it was dangerous for her son to make a half-day school visit to the power station at Trawsfynydd. Whatever the answers, it is usually impossible to put the minds of these callers completely at rest. Replacing Offa's Dyke with a lead shield is our usual attempt at a humorous response, while a more cynical thought is that Meibion Glyndwr should turn to propagandizing (in England) the levels of nuclear pollution in the language heartlands.

So I stared at the opposite coast and afterwards remembered the famous words in the Layfield Report, that document that has given the go-ahead to Britain's first PWR at Sizewell: 'I was not able to base my conclusions on a final safety case for Sizewell 'B', as none was submitted.' Here is another exercise in blind faith, a pious gesture that the CEGB and the Nuclear Inspectorate can be trusted not to allow a nuclear accident to happen. As far as this report is concerned, the Chernobyl disaster never occurred. Then our car lurched and we plummeted towards the ground, and all I had time to notice was my daughter's face, set and challenging, while her voice a moment later stated that next year she would be old enough to visit the waxworks and see the worst things in the world.

The Treatment

Theirs was a regular procession through the village. Usually ten, occasionally twenty people walked single-file up the hill to our large common, with its cotton-grass and tea-black pools of bogwater. Some moved with eyes cast down as if examin-ing the haydust and petrol rainbows on the road. Others looked around as if disturbed to see how far they had come. There were always leaders, men and women dressed differently from the others, whose pace would sometimes become too swift. Then they would pause, and sigh, and light a cigarette while waiting for the file of walkers to catch up and the slow, largely mute invasion to continue.

Such expeditions were so familiar that most people who lived in the village hardly seemed to notice. But I peered down from my bedroom window or through the leaves of a hedge, and found the shabby clothes, the expressions, the every movement of these passers-by, both alarming and extraordinary. Some whispered incomprehensibly to themselves; others, very occasionally, sang snatches of popular songs. One woman, with face and hair as pale as smoke, twisted her head to left and right like a periscope: while one man, immensely tall and with all possible colour bleached from his skin, crept insect-like onward. Every step looked as if it might be his last, but this ice-man continued unblinkingly up our street, eyes transparent as the feathery globes of thistle-heads, the bridge of his nose as long and sharp, it seemed to me, as a chisel. I never saw these people walking alone, and once in formation, they kept to their positions as if acting on instructions. As a child I compared them to the beads of an ugly necklace, threaded together by some shared, inexplicable torment. Sometimes I would hear women in the village speaking to the walkers as they paused on our steep hill. They always used the soothing, unlistening, unengaged voices normally reserved for children and animals.

These people were a different tribe that we sometimes tolerated in our midst.

Growing up, it was an irritation that I lived in a place associated for most outsiders, with mental illness. Three major hospitals lay on the outside of the village, providing employment for many of its residents. That in fact was the traditional joke. One half of the neighbours worked in the wards while the other half went there for treatment. Even now I occasionally meet comedians who after asking where I was brought up, enquire whether I'm still taking the tablets. The walkers who plodded through our streets were being given exercise, the sights of children and working men and women, the smells of hay-making and cooking dinners hopefully providing a form of therapy.

The largest of those hospitals is shortly to close. It is a huge, but from the main road, invisible Victorian edifice, built behind high walls on what was a remote common. Really it is a village in itself, the main corridor being over a quarter of a mile long, with a series of side passages and wards like boughs diverging from a great trunk. I know of no uglier or more visually daunting building. Once inside its doorway any individual is immediately shrunk into insignificance by the size of this fortress and the confusing possibilities of its passageways. Yet despite the alienation created by its monolithic architecture, the staff have always prided themselves on creating a family atmosphere for their charges. What I glimpse now when speaking to retired nurses in the village, is a genuine affection for this monstrous place and especially for those patients for whom it became home. This is especially ironic as it is now national health policy to close down as many of these hospitals as possible and filter their inhabitants back into the 'community', optimistically into the care of their real families. This is a fine ideal but contains of course huge impracticalities. A similar policy has been carried out in New York, with the result that there has been a significant increase in the population of homeless, disturbed, traumatized people. These had no families to return to, no one to administer medication, nobody outside an institutionalized social-worker network who cared about their existence. And there is also the painful fact that many families have been destroyed by the prolonged, unfathomable, often bizarre behaviour of a single schizophrenic member. For the strain on a household coping with the exhausting and obsessional nature of this illness is immense. Strangely, there still exists in some quarters the notion that this type of condition is a by-product of the 'creative' or 'artistic' mind. In reality schizophrenia is a terrifying destroyer of any form of creativity. It lays waste the imagination and can concentrate the ocean of thought into narrow, boiling channels that lead in an ever more intense manner, to nowhere. It is also the disintegrator of identity, the shatterer of the ego, a massive distorting influence on awareness of self and the world.

Schizophrenia is now treated with chemicals, but these can also create frightening problems. Consultant psychiatrists these days are seen by the uninitiated as glorified pill-dispensers. They interview a patient, are told about the behaviour of that person, and then suggest a dosage designed to mask any aberration. If the prescription is too conservative, little change will occur: but if, as often happens, an overdose is administered, the victim is rendered zombie-like, or effectively lobotomised, until the medication in the body is exhausted. This treatment is merely the use of a chemical straitjacket, and is very much a hit-or-miss affair. Occasionally, I would suggest, the sufferer is left in a worse predicament than before medical attention was given. The anaesthetizing of the imagination and a dousing of the eye's brightness are terrible consequences of our reliance on tablets, particularly when they are described as unfortunate side-effects of necessary treatment. To have to place a pill by someone's plate at dinner, to bring a tablet upstairs with a cup of tea, are grindingly depressing experiences when you know that the minute grains of these capsules are desiccating the unique and beloved qualities of the person you have dedicated yourself to help.

Equally dispiriting can be the visits to the hospitals' therapy units. It is true that today many social and industrial skills are taught in these places, but often adults can only play darts, daub water-colours over sugar-paper, hunch over basket weaving and crochet-work. Apart from the television and the tablets, it can appear that the twentieth century has never begun in these rooms. Ancient, aimless time-killing chores fill the spaces between meals. Activities are promoted for their own sake by a grimly outnumbered, dutiful, but unimaginative staff. Too often the atmosphere in such places is one of embittered torpor and burnt-out frustration. All that merit encouragement are the virtues of passivity. I once sat in such a unit and watched the men and women engage in their routines. Each had the drama of his or her own predicament lodged somewhere beyond a chemical-numbed imagination. Outside in the freshly-dug gardens grew a host of different flowering shrubs, their species' names emblazoned on plastic squares. A great rhododendron bush, leaves hard and shiny as wine-bottles, brushed the window. It was a dark, strangely ominous tree almost as old as the hospital itself. The sour elixir that fermented in its foliage fell to earth and slowly poisoned the soil. In its wide shade not a single other plant could prosper.

Sometimes recently I have taken a writing class in a nearby industrial town. One of the original members is a chemistry student who has composed poetry since childhood. She is not prolific or confident, but the little that she does produce has the qualities of concentration and imagistic power that are far removed from the usual class material. Her poems are like minerals from which a precious stone has not been quite extracted. Her sentences are uncut, unshaped, but diamond-hard, and the class likes nothing better than to hear this writer read her work aloud in her small but unfaltering voice. Everyone thinks they know what she is writing about, but no one is completely sure. This student has a history of mental problems that goes back to childhood, and many of the poems relate to these times. As our last term drew to a close, so her behaviour seemed to point to another breakdown. She would arrive late, silent, agitated and glossy with perspiration. Then, at our last scheduled meeting, she failed to appear.

Two months later I received a message that she was resident in a hospital three hundred miles away, taking tablets and undergoing electric convulsive therapy. This form of treatment I had always considered a barbarous reaction to mental illness, the type of thing we will shudder at when we look back in twenty years' time. But the student was pleased with what the electrodes had achieved for her. Contrary to my prejudice, the invisible current had not scoured every word of poetry from her brain. She was still constructing her dark, irregular verses. After that I stopped hearing from her, until a few weeks ago I attended a poetry reading at the Tate Gallery. Our room was crowded with people, but in the front row a familiar face caught my eye. I noticed the magpie-blue mascara, the modern scarf, a shining wire at wrist and throat. And looking at the polished stones of the woman's earrings, I remembered her poems' hardness, proof against the acid of schizophrenia and of her own durability to withstand the electrical pulse that passed through her brain. I was astonished by the new public strength of 'my' writer, and her assured tone. We walked under the vast canvasses of the Mark Rothko exhibition, where cinnabar bled into orange and underwater greens and blues turned each gallery into an aquarium. One huge picture was utterly black. We stood beneath its frame like travellers who had come to an unscalable cliff. A keeper padded up.

'When you're here all day,' he whispered, 'these paintings have a real emotional effect. They start to play on your mind.'

I felt myself taken aback. This was the first time I could remember a gallery warden giving an opinion of any kind. I had always viewed such people as car-park attendants for paintings, and suspected that they had long developed a sullen hatred of anything to do with art. The three of us stared at the blackness. There was nothing my mind could do with it: I felt myself refusing to enter its pit-like darkness, to be crushed by its huge gravity. The keeper went off softly.

'He killed himself,' my companion whispered. 'On the day these paintings were delivered to the Tate he slashed his throat. Or something like that.'

A little later she left the gallery and returned to her hospital.

A few days after this I visited an exhibition of medical history at the large hospital on the moor. I toured the waxworks of costumed nurses, fingered an assortment of hypodermics used throughout the century. There was a black box, rather bigger than a car-battery at the centre of the display. It was wound with old-fashioned flex and there was a variety of dials and switches relating to the size of the electrical charge the box generated. No one fully understands, said a notice, how electricity works in combating clinically-diagnosed depression, but there is no doubting its efficacy. In many cases, ECT has been a life-saver, and there are far fewer side-effects with modern electrical treatment than in the early stages of its development.

Outside in the gardens were the figures of another waxworks.

Men and women with nothing in their faces, nothing in their eyes but the ancient memory of a drug-dimmed obsession, walked beneath the sandstone turrets of their citadel. Tiny window panes like the bottoms of bottles gleamed along the walls. But though I hated the place I could not wish it out of existence. One in five people, said the leaflet in my hand, experience depression that requires treatment. Women are twice as likely as men to suffer from a diagnosed state of this illness. In a society that refuses to acknowledge the vast range of such problems, and consistently undervalues the worth of its caring professions, such resources that we have for helping those who need them are extremely precious, even when those facilities are Victorian relics isolated on a rough heath.

I thought of the student-poet, anaesthetized in her white shift, as the arrows leapt in the box beside her, and the current sliced through her brain. Abandoning herself to the barbarous lifesaver that no one really understands was an act of courage. It is possible that she will return to Wales next year, and bring back to her class the verse constructions that so puzzled and delighted her fellow members. And I also thought of the village where, Indian-file, the walkers still move in a ragged circle about the now smart estates where there used to be fields, the drained and sterile lawns that have replaced the purple common. The cars drive faster today, and the neighbours are strangers. All that has remained unchanged is the pace of that procession moving slowly up the hill.

Trespassers

The invitation card gleamed seductively. It promised a grand opening, free cocktails and historic surroundings. At the bottom in small gold letters, added as if an afterthought, was the motto of the old, now dissolved estate. On an accompanying brochure the hotel policy of encouraging conference and wedding parties was tastefully spelled out, and finally there was the signature of the Cardiff bookmaker who now owned the manor and its grounds.

Slowly, but inevitably, I found myself angered by his massive proletarian nerve. The man was announcing possession of something that could never belong to him. Didn't he know there were other claimants to that square mile of woods and streams and intricately laid-out manor gardens? Suddenly I was on the side of the nearly extinct species of aristocrat that had been forced to sell its family silver.

Trespassing, I am often told, is a civil offence. Prosecution is unlikely unless it can be proved that it is the trespasser's intention to cause damage. Where I was brought up, trespassing came as naturally as breathing. It had to, as most of the surrounding country was patrolled by farmers, gamekeepers and land-agents, determined to uphold the rights of private ownership. As all the most interesting territory was unpenetrated by public rights of way, I was forced to formulate a crude but effective governing philosophy. The land might belong to someone else, but it still remained my environment. And I was going to enjoy it. Usually it was one man who stood between me and the pleasures of exploration. A local gamekeeper haunted the rural no-go area that I had dedicated myself to discover, and it was his abiding principle that no-one should bend a wire or force a hedge and enter his domain.

I had good teachers. Sometimes I would accompany a boy my age, a dark and hyperactive poacher, on sorties into the estate.

Often our only motive was discovery, but occasionally we would stalk the pheasants that lived at wood margins and in the dangerous territories of gorse. These moved like huge golden cats through the long grass, remaining on the ground until their pursuers were within a step or two. I remember looking into the terrified eye of one of these birds we had almost unwittingly cornered. It was the most exotic creature I had ever seen, and the stupidest. Our only weapons were fern-shafts, complete with sickle-shaped roots, but the idea of assault was banished from my mind, at least, by the sight of the intricate feathers as orange as bracken, the pathetic and useless beauty of this over-bred inhabitant of the estate. Then the bird exploded at our feet and took to the air with a ridiculous corgi-like barking, and across the field we glimpsed the guardian of this doomed species coming towards us.

Looking back, it was an unequal contest. The man moved stiffly and was unable to run. Under a slouch-hat his face showed the unhealthy yellow sheen of elderwood, and wherever he ventured a pair of labradors the colour of church-brass nuzzled his hands. What was most exciting was the series of small gibbets he built around his cottage, displaying the carcasses of magpie and rabbit. This man killed things. Sometimes he would discover me fishing for loach and the bootlace-like eels in the stream that ran through the middle of the estate, and which felt to me at least, a most forbidden place. A favourite spot was where the brook emerged from a tunnel under the main South Wales railway line. Here the water was black as Turkish coffee and surrounded by treacherous silts. Heard from inside the tunnel, the steam-trains' whistles had an unearthly sound, like the cry of a peacock, and the passage of the carriages above put a tremor into the water, as if there was something invisible moving against the current. It was always when I heard that blast and felt the air and ground tremble, that I thought capture was imminent.

Usually I would see the gamekeeper as I crouched in spiky stems of archangel on this stream bank. He was a thin man who moved painfully, shotgun broken at his side. Really he and his dogs were not difficult to avoid. The gamekeeper was already old and carrying a cancer when I tormented him. One day he sat down in his woodshed and fired both barrels of the gun into his skull. I sometimes wondered if I had heard the actual detonation, that sent the pigeons up from the trees around his cottage, and set the dogs pacing their kennel-run.

The best part of trespassing was infiltrating the gardens of the mansion itself and creeping up to the house. A team of workmen looked after the seeding, mowing and hedging of the grounds, but they were easily avoided. Once I walked up the front steps, which were guarded by twin stone lions, and listened to a conversation in one of the drawing rooms. Its window seemed a huge garden-filled glass in which magnolias swayed and a lake shone. I pressed myself like a swallow to the wall and strained to catch the brief gusts of words. There was mortar in my eye and the vine of crimson ivy felt like ice against my cheek. I imagined the house as an enormous honeycomb of light and flame, full of astonishing secrets I would surely share. I pushed harder against the wall, becoming a stubborn ivy root, noticing how strongly that plant sucked against the stone, its stems leaving the surface scarred with marks like the white imprint of birds' feet. This was an extraordinary feeling, a sensing of some otherness, the existence of a new and different life. The mansion house, and what existed around and inside it, seemed to lure the imagination like some shy animal, out into the sun. I sidled off through a maze of flowering shrubs, each ticketed with a Latin name. Now I was powerful, a rapt discoverer, and the fact of my own trespassing undiscoverable.

Getting caught, I would immediately offend again. Often the territory I invaded was a ramshackle farm in the middle of the village and kept by two formidably dishevelled child-haters. Today there is asphalt over the orchards, and usually a rank of Ford Sierras, each with a neat business suit on a hanger in the back window, parked where the greengage trees used to be. Their windscreens are speckled with orange insect-blood. The farm is now a country pub, and I sometimes drink its expensive beer under one of the garden's plastic parasols. Somewhere around here there used to be a well. Looking down at it as a child, the water had glinted like birchbark. And in the stone front room of the farm I had once found the two old men asleep amongst flagons and cats, a large cheese on the table before them luxuriant with blue moss. For generations many of the people of the village had worked on the surrounding estate. Most of the others were cheerful lifelong trespassers, and that division has been preserved in the new pub. For the lounge is now known as 'The Gamekeepers' Bar', and the public room, 'The Poachers'. Before the house was brought into the sanitary age there had been only one waterless latrine on the farm, a chicken-coop with two holes cut in a wooden seat. Investigating one morning, I came upon the two ancient residents squatting there like broad and cumbersome Toby jugs, each clutching a handful of straw. They knew who I was and where I lived. I was aware that I might easily escape any challenge or pursuit they offered. But there was always the threat of the slurry-pit. This was an unfathomable olive-green bog located in a large open-topped stone sty. In very dry weather the local children dared to walk over its crust, which was always slightly yielding, and sometimes ominously creaked. In rain it turned to soup, and we would watch the sticks and pebbles placed on its surface slowly submerge in the steaming morass. So it was the prospect of being pitched into the slurry that I took home with me that morning, and which might have dampened the trespassing urge for a few days.

Today the farmhouse has every convenience. The women's toilet is labelled 'hens' and the men's 'cocks'. After they sold the house and barns the farmers moved to separate cottages. Beili Mawr was renovated and calling in for a drink during the new pub's opening week, one of them achieved the distinction of being refused service and turned away from his old, now unrecognisable front door. Wild hair and broken corduroy would not sit well beneath the swaying parasols. A different sort of trespasser had moved in and was busy establishing its own regime of video games and toasted sandwiches.

I fingered the invitation card in my pocket. Scores of vehicles surrounded the mansion house, parked on floodlit gravel. I had not been here for years and arrived this time by a legitimate route. There were no trespassers now, only inheritors and contenders, each bearing a white paper with four golden words in Welsh: *Gwell Angau Na Chywilydd* (Better Death Than Shame). We sat at tables and stood against a bar of magnificent hardwood. There were silver bowls with paper flowers. I talked a little but listened more as the guests slowly unlocked identities. The men were fluent, sporting and monied, erecting in easy speech their own ideas of themselves. These were the dealers in almost certainties, the well-groomed banishers of doubt. Usually the women were more silent, proud yet ultimately obedient, and lustrous as dragonflies. Some slight amusement played about their mouths, as if they were party to a private joke or watched over an inheritance. Sheathed knives.

I wondered if these were the people I had listened to years earlier as I hid against the mansion wall. But many were the families of workers on the old estate, the grown-up children of laundrywomen and gardeners, relaxing in hard-earned finery and re-sponsible for their own success. And of course it was only our custom at the bar that made us welcome. This time I stood on the other side of the wall, almost obliviously exchanging the secrets that once had seemed worth stealing. For trespassing is about belonging and not belonging. It is an exploration of ways in which you might, or might not, wish to live. It is about not feeling easy, or quite at home. Anywhere. Above all it is a state of mind that means you prefer borrowing to owning, moving to staying, and ensures a restless appetite for stepping, however uncertainly, over the line.

Not the Shell Guide

Tuesday

I join the queue and listen to those ahead place their orders. The girls behind the counter scoop pasties and fritters from the warming shelves, and roll the shoe-sized fish encased in rigid orange batter into newspaper. The great vat of dark oil, as large, it seems, as a small mountain pool, bubbles ferociously before us.

At the tables, teenagers crumple drink cans and mime to the juke-box. An old man pushes a ridiculously long, yellow chip into his mouth. But I look at the wall and read the posters. Above the dimpled vinegar bulbs and easi-squeez sauce bottles, James Joyce surveys the cafe between two pillars of Ulysses. George Bernard Shaw's beard has turned to steam, making him almost invisible. Like some ascetic dictator, Beckett condemns our frivolous, physical appetites.

Taking my food to the stone sea-wall I am surprised at my own reaction to a series of literary posters. This, after all, I tell myself, is another country. They do things differently and possibly better here. There might be poetry readings in the fishbar every Friday, whilst in the fizzing amusement arcades, perhaps the children turn occasionally from their huge, coffin-sized and -shaped video machines, to discuss Yeats's prosody, knowing that the poet is already in town, 'The Second Coming' bejewelled with tiny droplets of fat, spelled out above black and yellow check formica.

Possessed of the comforting illiteracy of the newcomer, I can read the signs as I wish. But as a temporary refugee from a land anaesthetized by jock-strap culture, where the occasional tacky wine-bar is dedicated to the false rumour of a poet's life and never his work, it is easy for me to feel this shock, a sudden surge of optimism. The juggernaut has obviously not rolled over everything. And one of the places still holding out is a chip shop in the resort of Bray, ten miles south of Dublin. Through the window I watch one of the plump waitresses wiping with her sleeve a great clean arc of daylight over the face of J.M. Synge.

Wednesday

At dawn I wake in the back of the car. A party of Germans has arrived in a minibus, and from beneath two sleeping bags I see them stamp their hiking boots on the asphalt and unfold plastic-covered maps. They disappear in the opposite direction I wish to take.

Glendalough is a powerful place. A dramatic glacial cleft occupied by two lakes, it retains even now a sense of remote sanctuary that must have appealed to the Celtic monk Kevin when he founded a monastery here in the sixth century. The only food I have left is a cardboard-stiff peanut-butter sandwich, yet before I leave, I make one last journey through the trees to a waterfall near where Kevin built his hut.

The information for visitors is bilingual and discreet, but soon I am beyond the suggested paths, and clinging to alder-roots and branches above an astonishing green cataract. Here, there is a deep, almost perfectly round bowl into which the water pours in fury. And yet the surface of the pool is undisturbed. It absorbs the energy of the mountain river and infuses it with the secrets of placid, immeasurable depth. Terrified, as a child, so I am told, of water, and now a belligerently ignorant non-swimmer, I am yet tempted to break the dazzling meniscus of the corrie, to shut myself in with the powers of this place. On either side, boulders the size of houses are covered by ivy trunks. Each ivy stem, like a millipede, clings with countless feet to the rock. If I dared, I would drink. Instead I snap ridiculously, like a dog, at the monsoon of spray from this vertical torrent.

Thursday

Dublin smells of money. The unmistakable odour persists in its ornate suburbs and varnished taverns, around the parks and the huge glass emporia, doused always in a glaring Mediterranean indoor light. This is the smell that my own country lacks, that perhaps only ever existed in the heyday of its docklands. It is damp and animal, growing ranker in the mind. Picking an iris leaf in a Dublin garden, I break it in two. And again smell money as I rub the leaf to wet, green shreds, coaxing out the meaty, excremental aroma. In this city it infuses everything.

I look down from the shop at the expressionless people in a famous street. In my hands the picture-book exhibits portraits of the new Irish. Four lean, male faces, stubbled, pitted, greyly melancholic, surely too young to have experienced what they already seem to know. The photographs are enormous and distorted, stretched like continents on a world map. These men are musicians and songwriters. Their lyrics are printed on the creamy paper, uneasy fragments of mystical, sexual verse, exhausted by the cruelty of the page.

Women perfumed with money wait in the nave of books. The staff, like suitors, surround them, eager for warmth at the fire of their silks and jewellery. The air is full of the music of the thin men, an electric, devotional frenzy that perhaps Kevin heard in his cell near the waterfall. Around us the volumes are stacked in pillars like the broken columns of a monastery. Serious, completely silent, the archaeologists inspect a ruin.

Friday

South Clare, with its marshy commons, coal workings and pitted roads is familiar country to anyone who knows the north of Glamorgan and Gwent. Apparently the Gorbachevs have recently visited the district, husband discussing 'modern issues' with the Irish premier, whilst wife was taken to the Bunratty Folk Park, 'where the past is present', to examine peasant customs and lament the almost complete absence of traditional Irish recipes for cheese.

The garage owner in Ballyvaughan sees a Welsh sticker on the back of the car and starts to talk. His education, he says, had all been done through the Irish language. It was the law. Which is bloody funny, because a hundred years previously, it was illegal even to be heard speaking Irish. Laws and languages don't mix, he claims. 'No one in north Clare speaks Irish now, anyway. But you'll hear the students using it in Galway, and if you go on further to Connemara...'

What he doesn't like is Radio Gaeltacht, or the people featured on its programmes. 'They sometimes come here for petrol, and they're arrogant bastards. And on the radio, why don't they speak slower or use some English words? They're purists, just doing their own thing. But that's nothing compared with the Irish service from Dublin. Christ, did you ever hear such an accent? The programmes are shit, you can't speak Irish with an accent like that.'

Last night in a bar in Ennistymon that also doubled as the town undertaker's parlour, an advert had been screened exhorting people to use the language. A handful of sullen farmers sipped bitter in the gloom. Their accents were so pronounced it was difficult to understand their conversation, but one claimed that because even English grammar had been taught to him through Irish, he 'had to learn everything twice'.

Saturday

On my right, the Burren is a frozen ocean. To the left, the Atlantic seems a dark green slab of marble, the occasional tiny beach a scallop of orange sand. But I have no time for the sea view, for here in the north of Clare is one of the most puzzling landscapes in these islands.

It is a world of stone, treeless and almost grassless, the grey plateaux interrupted by eroding pinnacles, rounded peaks and summits littered with huge boulders. I drive, then walk for miles inland, and the Burren becomes higher, stranger. It is almost dusk, and the silhouettes of megaliths, looking as if they might have been constructed yesterday, suddenly loom over a wall or dominate a bend. Any farming would seem impossible here, but tiny fields of a few square yards have been painstakingly picked clean of the torrential scree, and enclosed by tall, beautifully joined dry stone walls.

There are flowers too in abundance. Spiky orchids and gentians unique to this desert flourish in crevices, in tufts between boulders and the rare patches of turf. And there are tombs of forgotten races on the highest plains of rock, gaunt monuments almost indistinguishable from the natural formations. From a gate a hooded crow observes me as I pass. I note the claspknife beak and limestone-coloured surplice. The Irish bird of bad omen holds its ground, then clatters off, its voice matching the territory.

Travelling north the rock becomes less abundant. There are black peatbogs now, topped with pale moor grass, and then suddenly, the White Castle Hotel. I stop to look at this creation. The only other buildings for miles have been modest bungalows and even smaller thatched and whitewashed huts, each with its conical hayrick and tethered goat. But the White Castle is enormous, an Irish version of a Disneyland idea of a medieval fortress. In a country of a thousand ruined towers, and in one of its bleakest corners, here is a Hollywood film-set, its breeze-block turrets and courtyards newly built and already flaking, a castellated nightclub on the yellow common. Guinevere should now appear, clutching a hamburger. I drive along the empty road away from this mirage.

Sunday

The Shell Guide to Ireland was co-written by Lord Kilannin, who started work on the book in 1947. This month sees the first updated version in twenty-two years. It is easy to tell what attracts his lordship's ire. Even in the Burren, bungalows are springing up, usually very low and very long, whitepainted, with large gravel gardens and ridiculously intricate iron gates. From the history-soaked authenticity of his own mansion, Kilannin describes such developments as 'atrocious'.

Whether the Irish are building such homes for themselves is doubtful. Here on the west coast, the talk and the newspapers are full of emigration. The UK and USA are as ever the goals, and there is with the latter an ironic exchange of highly educated but unemployed young people for middle-aged American tourists exploring their roots.

This week, the *New York Times* has published a full-page guide to the city of Galway. I wake here at dawn in a steamed-up car on the Corrib Wharf. Below me in the harbour, sixty swans glide amongst rowing-boats, whilst seals turn their heads like periscopes a little above the surface.

Last night in Taaffe's, in *An Pucan* and the other bars, I joined the Germans and Americans in search of music. Every tavern in the capital of the west boasts the authentic sound of fiddles and tin whistles. Whether what we heard was brilliant or mediocre is difficult to tell, but I did note the sweat of the florid ensembles, together with the unflinching determination of the young men of the town to drink themselves as quickly into oblivion as possible. Despite the craft shops, the new restaurants, the literary and academic culture here, the history and present wealth, Galway remains a drinking town.

Moving through the Spanish Steps I eventually discover the city's main square, a magnificent space surrounded by arbitrary sculpture. It is too early for most people to be travelling to work, but I am immediately approached by a beautiful Jehovah's Witness, immaculate in dress and dogma. Unshaven and head thickened by Guinness, I hope my politeness makes a good start to her day. She is consulting with colleagues in a corner of the park as I move off in search of breakfast.

Monday

Rain in Limerick and a macadam-dark Shannon, Cadbury's chocolate in Thurles, completely different from the stuff made in Britain, coffee and oddly pleasant exhaustion in Kilkenny. On the ferry I already miss the *Irish Times*, the monstrous churches and the bookshops so important to the community. Ennis is known as the capital of Clare, but it has a population of only six thousand and no university. Yet its bookshop commands the town, and boasts a huge stock of works by Irish writers. At Duty Free I join the queue, but not even the bargain Jamesons, in its Atlantic- coloured plastic, will be potent enough to bring back the taste of the place.

Feeding the Baby

Sometimes there is nothing to see. Often it is difficult to understand what I am looking for. The town of Bray, ten miles south of Dublin, is quiet under its gorse-yellow hill with a range of mountains towering beyond. It is still early in the season and only a few people are to be seen outside Casey's Casino and Dawson's Amusement Arcade. Beneath the cliff the cormorants' rock is noisy as a schoolyard, and these birds, black as friars, mingle with sleeker, red-footed divers on the skerries.

There is an idea of opulence here, a faded, forgotten gentility. But behind the serene terraces the local supermarket has achieved national prominence this week, the newspapers full of an incident in which baby-food bought in the store was found to contain slivers of glass. I hear the few local people I pass discussing the incident. The whole country seems full of a strange paranoia, and even in the bars the drinkers stop their gossip as the televisions parade psychologists who seek to explain the saboteurs' motives.

On the headland path I listen to the conversation of the couple ahead. Travelling alone, after days sometimes hardly speaking, it is easy to become involved with the banal asides of strangers. They mention contaminated land in the mountains beyond the resort, unexploded bombs and various spilled poisons around a deserted army camp. Then they stop and point to the bays in the south, fingers slowly moving north to where a distant ferry is approaching harbour. The coast they are gesturing at, quite invisible from here, must be that of Wales, and at the furthest extreme of their interest, Cumbria. Their tone is a mixture of resignation and anger, and from ten yards away I can hear every word.

Reluctantly I leave Bray, the clear waters off its breakwater the grey-green colour of a computer screen. A day later I am on North Bay, south of Blackwater. This is a strange coastline of dunes and thatched cottages, and small travelling fairs seemingly marooned in lay-bys or ramshackle caravan parks. Again there are few people. At noon I count three other walkers on a four-mile expanse of yellow-white sand. The only sounds are the waves and a cuckoo in the woods behind the thick marram. But when the wind is in the grass, it hums like the wires of electricity pylons.

I think of the sands at home, in their own ways no less impressive, their dune-systems even larger and more rugged. There the sea-borne plastics are piled up in great moraines along the high-tide margins. Dig down a few inches into the beaches and you encounter the cans and bottles and rust-devoured aerosols of earlier years. Gouge further and reach other detritus, deeper now than the roots of the sea-holly that Shakespeare knew as an aphrodisiac, and which Alun Lewis thought the bluest of all blue flowers. On those shores old gas canisters stand on the beach like torpedoes, while in my home resort until recently, two outfall pipes pumped untreated human waste and contraceptives into the tide. If I bathed in the sea two hundred yards in front of my house I could anoint myself with my own diluted sewage.

But on North Bay there seems nothing like that. On my knees in the sand, running it carefully through my fingers, I do not discover the minute granules of indestructible polystyrene, or the plastic components of disposable nappies and sanitary towels that are inescapable on the beaches at home. Remarkably, impossibly it seems, this is a clean beach, cleaner even than the western shores of this country. Indeed standing three days earlier on the sands below the great limestone plateaux of the Burren in County Clare, looking towards the Aran Islands, it was astonishing to remember that the next land was three thousand miles away. And yet, at my feet, the marks of civilization were all too apparent. A jumble of bleached yet eternal plastics, anonymous artefacts of ship or town life worn smooth as pebbles, had been brought here on the tide to one of the most remote stretches of shoreline in Ireland.

Now, on the other side of the country, I look at the pale sand. Like a parent suspecting fragments of glass in baby-food, I wonder about the pollution that is not visible. At the nuclear reprocessing plant at Sellafield in Cumbria, scientists admit that one third of a tonne of plutonium has been deposited in the Irish Sea, which is consequently the most radioactively contaminated stretch of ocean in the world. Sellafield is closer to Dublin than it is to London. The same scientists claim that because of marine dispersal and dissolution, such emissions are harmless. Plans to locate another Pressurized Water Nuclear Reactor at Yr Wylfa on Ynys Môn have drawn official protests from the Irish government, and a large outcry from pressure groups in the Republic, including Greenpeace which since 1987 has had an office in Dublin.

Already the *Irish Medical Journal* has publicised higher than average rates of leukaemia and other cancers on the east coast of Ireland. The 1957 fire at Windscale (now Sellafield) which was kept secret by the British authorities until recently, is thought to be responsible for the high incidence of Down's Syndrome babies born to mothers who lived around Dundalk, which is on the coast directly opposite the reprocessing works. Meanwhile, Sellafield continues to pour millions of gallons of radioactive water into the Irish Sea.

Ireland is one of only two countries in the European Community that dumps sewage sludge at sea. The other is the UK. Around the coast of Wales there are over two hundred outfall pipes that take human effluent into estuaries or directly offshore. About eighty of these pump raw sewage. A further thirty-six release 'trade waste' which can contain a huge variety of pollutants, including boiled- down material from abattoirs.

One of these pipelines is located at Llanina Point near Aberaeron. Working at maximum rate, this outlet could release 130,000 gallons of 'screened and macerated' sewage into Cardigan Bay every day. (Screening is the process of removing plastics and sanitary items from the effluent. Maceration is the chopping up of the waste and its dousing with chlorine.) Meanwhile, in southwest Wales, over 25,000,000 gallons of human sewage are poured every day into the rivers between the Neath and the Gwendraeth Fach. A good deal of this pollution obviously flows into the sea.

Confronted by such figures it is hard not to sympathize with Irish outrage at marine pollution, although it must be admitted that the country's own sea-dumping policy contributes to the fouling of its own shores. It is even more difficult, however, to tolerate the bland assurances of British bureaucrats when the problems of such pollution are presented to them. I personally treasure a letter from a private secretary of Mr Peter Walker who wrote to me that '...the discharge of properly screened and macerated sewage through long outfalls that are properly designed, sited, constructed and maintained is a perfectly acceptable method of disposal.'

Long outfalls work on the principle of short outfalls. This is that the sea is an infinite waste-disposal unit, capable of neutralizing every toxin we can throw into it. Like a magician's box, it makes things miraculously disappear. Long outfalls merely pump the waste we create into out-of-sight areas of the sea. If built on the west coast of Wales, Ireland will presumably receive even larger amounts of our sewage. Meanwhile, most people have to put up with cracked and broken short outfalls which leave on our own beaches what we thought we had flushed away for ever.

Ireland also has to put up with the effects of the rubbish that is pumped into estuaries such as the Mersey. 7,000,000 tonnes of chemically polluted dredge spoil from here is deposited in the Irish Sea every year, together with 4,000,000 tonnes from other estuaries. This is on top of the 2,000,000 tonnes of industrial waste and 2,000,000 tonnes of sewage sludge tipped annually into the sea between Britain and Ireland.

In fact, the Mersey can claim to be Europe's most polluted estuary. Two hundred companies based around its banks are allowed, by government exemption from prosecution, to discharge waste. One of these pumps over five hundred tonnes of ammonia each year into the river, together with another thirty tonnes of cancer-linked chemicals. At Port Sunlight, factories making soap and washing powder have released their waste into the estuary since 1888 with almost complete immunity from prosecution and even control.

There's an odd kind of environmental imperialism in our use of the seas as a place to hide the unpleasant by-products of our society. These are the areas of the planet which we may treat in any way we think fit. Questions of personal or national responsibility have rarely arisen, because, like the atmosphere, the sea has had no actual value placed on it by our civilization. The 'long outfall pipes' are rather like the 'taller chimney' answers of those who dismiss the effects of air pollution. The problem, I suppose, is that we still tend to look on parts of the planet, especially the oceans, the rainforests and Antarctica, as acres so vast that there is nothing we can do that can harm them. In reality, the technology that makes life comfortable and worthwhile for most of us has reduced the world to a small, highly vulnerable, already damaged piece of real estate. Yet Western man still operates as if the wilderness started outside his front door or the gate of his factory. The truth is it doesn't exist any more.

One of the more interesting 'solutions' to this dilemma that I have encountered comes from the Centre for Incentive Taxation. To cut levels of air pollution and thereby the greenhouse effect and damage to the ozone layer, countries should treat the atmosphere above their land surfaces as taxable areas. If a company pollutes this atmosphere in any way, then it should pay a heavier tax than those companies that do not pollute. Jokes about the government making us pay for the air we breathe might now follow thick and fast. The oceans, at least around our own shores, might be treated similarly.

When I stand on the beaches of South Wales and look at the seawater, it is usually impossible to describe it other than a frothy grey soup. Recently the M.P. for the Vale of Glamorgan made an indignant speech in the Commons after he had witnessed local lifeguards emerge from a training session 'covered in human waste'. The only remarkable thing about this was John Smith's outrage. Had he never bathed in the area, or listened to the complaints of thousands of residents of Barry and Aberthaw?

But crouching now on the white flank of the bays south of Black- water and looking into the ocean shallows, I feel only surprise at the clarity, the lack of foreign bodies here. All beaches, in a way, are great excremental deserts, made vulnerable and yet protected by the ruling tides. Behind me in the small villages of the coast whole families are walking together to church. The hymns, caught faint on the wind, sound like the whispers of the reed beds between the thatched houses and the dunes. I cannot see anything in the water. Perhaps once more I have forgotten what I am looking for. Occasional shops in the deserted squares have opened for trade. I stopped at one earlier for milk and the newspapers. There was going to be a general election, the gossip said; the Irish soccer team was on the up-and-up, and wouldn't it be a damn good thing when they caught the maniacs who were putting the tiny, invisible pieces of glass into jars of baby-food.

Demo

Morning

8.45 a.m. There are twelve of us in the hired van that circulates the avenues of government buildings and private offices. Suddenly the navigator jabs his finger and we cross the wide street into a car-park. The barrier is up and the tarmac deserted.

'How the hell can we have missed it?' curses the driver, reversing savagely into the empty road. As everyone else feels no responsibility for any of the organization of the trip, we keep silent, and soon are speeding back past the ornate banks and graceful finance houses of The Hague.

My teeth feel like moist cardboard, while the heart is a greyhound after the last transfusion of black coffee. On the ferry over, our cabin was so far beneath the decks that I was convinced I could hear the North Sea sliding in icy planes three inches below my bunk. The cabin was free. No pillow, no blanket, only an assortment of plastic mattresses. I awoke this morning with one of the seams imprinted on my cheek and my clothes soaked with perspiration and the lager someone had poured over me in the wildly tilting bar. Food is a concept almost comically remote.

9.10 a.m. Now the streets are full of young men in impeccable suits. Through the grime on the window we watch the dazzling office girls make orderly progress down the cycle lanes. The music of the photocopier and the elevator becomes the morning's soundtrack, and as the van pulls up in the forecourt of a tasteful, garden-skirted high-rise, we glimpse two figures with coloured placards. We have found our demonstration.

10.00 a.m. You cannot argue with the banners and leaflets. No one disputes the information on our handouts. Hurrying between bank and office the Dutch do not blink an eye as we ask them to think about the statistics we quote in our strange accents. Every

99

minute of every day one hundred acres of the world's tropical rainforests are destroyed. Every day an uncalculated number of species become extinct. Perhaps a cure for cancer or a cure for Aids was lost this minute. Forever. Soil erosion, climatic change, the nurturing of deserts, the destruction of the world's genetic reservoir. Before we start speaking double Dutch we break for tea and pastries down the road.

10.30 a.m. In the restaurant I think of a video I have seen recently. It features an Indonesian hunter who makes his living trapping Sumatran tigers and selling their pelts, bones and meat to various dealers. The skins finish up in the Far East fashion industry, while the bones are ground into powder and sold as aphrodisiacs and medicines. The film shows him skilfully trapping one of these animals and peeling it like some golden fruit. It was sad, he said. There were no tigers left. Soon he would have no way of earning a living and his children would starve. Asked why he had helped hunt the Sumatran tiger into oblivion, the man looked baffled. It was the only thing he could do, he answered. There was no other way of existing.

11.00 a.m. We are in The Hague to lobby delegates of the World Bank on Indonesia's 'Transmigration' policy. This is the forcible removal of millions of Indonesians from over-populated islands such as Java to rainforested areas occupied by smaller groups of tribal peoples. This process means the destruction of the forests, the obliteration of the tribal cultures they maintained, and in-calculable misery for the millions forced into exile in inhospitable terrain. The World Bank funds this operation as it pays for the construction of gargantuan dam-systems in the Amazon, schemes carried out with the minimum of interest in the environmental and human consequences.

Thus our van-load of respectful English, Welsh and Australian citizens stands with our leaflets and watches the delegates from over one hundred of the world's countries arrive to lobby for the billions of dollars the World Bank is putting up for grabs. These gentlemen (I see no women) wander in relaxed fashion towards the entrance, most of them graciously accepting our literature. Some of them seem to think we are part of an international welcoming committee. These are important people with first-class air tickets and heavy schedules. Every item on their huge agenda will affect the world in some way for years to come. One of the Indonesian party, unused perhaps to even the politest demonstrations, demands that the police move us on. An officer strolls across, strokes his holster, and in excellent English gives us a warning about our future behaviour as the delegates converge on the rosewood tables and mahogany toilet seats of their conference rooms. I feel so fragile and uncertain that I cannot imagine posing a threat to anyone, but our group, while not looking quite like rent-a-mob, does have a wild-eyed and ferry-lagged appearance.

Afternoon

3.30 p.m. We visit the nearest supermarket for provisions. Heaped up with orange juice, bananas, coffee, chocolate, bread, eggs, pills, we push our trolley through the rainforest. In consumerland it is difficult enough to remember that bacon comes from pigs and potatoes from the earth, without puzzling over the sources of the wooden shelves and household fittings in the next-door DIY department, the veneers, the chipboard, the panelling, the patio-doors, the bathroom cabinets that seem somehow to have been spirited into vaguely aromatic, plastic-sheathed existence.

The Dutch shops are packaged in synthesizer music and acres of glass. Their names and the goods they sell, are, however, immediately familiar to all our group. Apart from the absence of litter in the streets and graffiti on the walls, we might be in Cardiff or Manchester. Diversity is richness, we like to say with the poets and the philosophers, and yet we inevitably participate in a consumer system which is now accomplishing the greatest and most thorough destruction of cultures, habitats and species the world has ever experienced. A combination of ignorance and appetite has created this new Ice Age. In the time it takes to walk down one of the polished aisles of this citadel of commerce, another one hundred acres of rainforest are levelled. During the period it needs to fill our trolley with rainforest bounty, two thousand acres of the habitat that originally produced it are reduced to a naked layer of topsoil that can survive a maximum of three years cropping before becoming desert.

4.00 p.m. During the afternoon our crowd is swollen by Dutch citizens for whom, of course, any Indonesian issue is of some significance. Exiles from Papua New Guinea bring music and banners and an angry urgency to the day. Indonesia's expansion here, and also from island to island in the Timor Sea is denounced by a succession of speakers and singers. One of the world's forgotten wars is surfacing briefly in the diplomatic gardens of The Hague.

We camp on the square until the end of the working day, giving out leaflets and repeating the numbing statistics. A member of the Dutch cabinet arrives, holds a brief press conference and departs. Transmigration, it seems, is to go on being supported by the World Bank, which will provide perhaps $80,000,000 for the next year. I think of the hunter's razor making its tiny incision below the tiger's anus, and the slow blade travelling through the belly's pale fur. We eat oranges and drink coffee and the representatives of one hundred foreign offices make a soundless descent past the smoked plate glass of the ministry and board their luxury coaches at the back of the building. The Papuans remain, beating drums and waving flags of independence, as the secretaries start to emerge, followed by the immaculate suits and post-impressionist ties. The music of the afternoon becomes the whirring of bicycle spokes.

For a few minutes the whole day appears as a blur of futility. I remember a march in Cardiff, a tremendous procession of humorous and concerned people showing their resentment at plans to build a Pressurized Water Reactor at Hinkley Point. The rain fell in warm torrents on all of us, but especially it seemed on a friend's child who was accompanying our party for the day. It blossomed in his hair and lay like jewellery around the neck of his shirt. As he trailed his wafer-like daps through the scummy gutters of St Mary Street I laughed at his expression, but mine was an uneasy emotion. Touching him, he oozed like a sponge. Something in that stern, bright face said he would not be doing this again.

Evening

7.00 p.m. I doubt if I would enjoy the rainforest. I think of a sauna crawling with malevolently-coloured insects, a shrinking stage that holds the world's evolutionary prima donnas, each determined to make the most bizarre impact before the theatre is demolished. Someone at the ministry with me this morning stated that after spending two years with a tribe in Venezuela he arrived back in Britain with seventeen separate tropical diseases. Yet the truth is that while our lives depend on the rainforest's continued existence, our lifestyles ensure its destruction. In actual global size it has shrunk by half since the last war – forty years to destroy what took seventy million years to develop. If present rates of obliteration are maintained, everything will be lost by about 2030.

An obvious fact is that we do not know what we are losing. Every day species of plants and animals unrecorded by science become extinct. They make up the planet's invisible natural history. Sometimes in schools I show slides of a tribe of Amazonian Indians, a family group smiling shyly at the camera. The photograph was the work of the first person from outside the rainforest those people had encountered. It was taken about six years ago, and it is difficult to think optimistically about life for the tribe after that moment of history and the end of innocence. Out there, in the final unexplored niches of Peru and Brazil, the last people in the world not to wear tee-shirts await the fatal contact.

Midnight

Amsterdam was a neon rainforest full of people dreamy-eyed with its tropical substances. We sat in flickering bars, then drove back to the ferry-port. Now on board, we watch a cabaret group sing standards from a madly swaying stage, while Dutch Hell's Angels and English soccer fans bawl tribal slogans at each other. This time I make up a bed on the floor, my coat pockets still bulging with leaflets. Meanwhile the tiger hangs from a wire in a clearing of the forest and the air thrums like a photocopier as the flies descend on the few pieces of offal the hunter cannot use. This full-grown male has shrunk to a thin baby, red with crying. His great feet, once striped and soft as forest orchids, are now thin beaks of muscle. The hunter seems to be pulling the tail inside out, so that finally its pelt hangs loose, like a sleeve. And at last it is free, the precious skin, wholly free of the ridiculous carcass with its pinched child's face and narrow beam of backbone. So the shadows and the sunlight of the tiger's fur are rolled up like a sleeping-bag, and the hunter pads off with his extinct skill, satisfied for the moment, into the trees.

Dock of the Bay

Sometimes, only mildly maliciously, I ask friends in the capital whether they've been to the beach recently. They usually shrug and name a South Wales resort or two. Then the malice becomes superiority: 'But haven't you been to the beach at Cardiff?' There's no reply to this but the puzzled 'There is no beach at Cardiff.'

I then let my eyebrows do the talking. Dropping them a millimetre implies that this is an assertion of amazing yet all too typical ignorance. Persist, and there's a risk of having your know-it-all block knocked off. The conversation usually ends with a map drawn on a beer-mat and some instructions.

The idea is to get yourself out to Rover Way, off Newport Road, now dominated by the big, heartbreaking sheds of DIY companies. Drive or cycle past the Bird Brothers scrap metal empire, which in the years since I worked there, seems to have flourished. There are now peaks of twisted iron and steel that loom with a Snowdonian ruggedness over the flat khaki of Tremorfa. The yard looks to have grown by about an acre, and the small prefabs with their year-round Christmas decorations and yellow cartridges of rat poison extended to a real office, at least something that looks habitable. There might even be women there now, not merely the biro-decorated pullouts from skin magazines.

I spent a winter there doing ledger work, weighing in and out gypsy-driven transits filled up with exhaust systems and ancient plumbing, and then bigger stuff, shuddering DAFs and Leyland trucks that left a film of diesel soot over the weighbridge cabin, a sticky fallout like the unburnt gunpowder in dead fireworks. I sat by a radiator so hot it would take the skin off your fingers, impaling one docket after another on the spike. Stuck there all day, using a clumsy adding machine called a comptometer and barking knees against the dynamite boxes stored in the bogs, one of the few anticipatory perks was the unscheduled arrival of either owner.

As far as I knew there were two Birds. Perhaps there still are. One motored round in a blackcurrant-coloured Rolls Corniche with a cream roof. The other had something luxurious. They would drive right into the yard and park by the precious-metal shop. Overhead would swing the shears, an expensive, mechanical vulture, that grabbed and tore scrap-cars to pieces, whilst along the oily paths glistening with swarf between the iron scree, and away from the tracks of the dangerously-silent locos that ran to and from East Moors steel-works, art-students, tolerated with amusement or exasperation, like some defective relation you don't see very often, would search for sculpture parts.

When the Birds arrived I kept out of the way, feeling the atmosphere's delicious tension, and watched Tudor, our manager, organise coffee on his tin-topped desk. The inside of every mug was stained ochre by years of only desultory swills. Not that the brothers seemed to mind. Flicking mud off expensive, pointed toes, they draped their overcoats on the safe and chewed the fat with the senior crew, a secret language as far as I was concerned. But all the same, every conversation I overheard contained lots of noughts. And now as you travel Rover Way, it looks as if the Birds are adding to them.

But read the beermat, and the instructions will tell you, don't stop just here. Keep on until you see the painted barrier of British Associated Ports at the entry to Cardiff Docks. Instead of going inside, look for the signs on the left that say 'Foreshore Road', and 'Heliport'. There might be a barrier across the entrance, but don't let it turn you back. Foreshore Road runs for a pointless quarter of a mile and ends in a turning circle. Walk up the bank, and from there you have a spectacular view towards Newport in the east and Penarth in the west. And below, Cardiff's iron beaches, lapped by the Orchard Ledges area of a Bristol Channel that scuttles to your feet like a beaten dog. Its waters are the colour of an unwashed cup.

Here really is an iron shore. Over the years industry has used this coast as the most convenient dumping ground for embarrassing waste. Black slag, blocks of asbestos like frozen smoke, ossified rivulets of sludge, boulders of sullen conglomerates slashed by curious gleaming veins, dram-loads of ore the colour of dried blood, paler flux, incomprehensible tangles of piping have all been cast away here, and now form briefly-intriguing, foot-wrenching strata for the explorer if not the ecologist. It's a country that looks and feels like a disintegrating brillo-pad. And it goes on for miles. You won't wish to stay long, or get your toes wet in the flayed sea. But before departing, note the sign in Foreshore Road stating this area is under surveillance and fly-tippers or vandals will be prosecuted. So look around as you leave for the invisible guardians of Cardiff's ironic beach.

Such pollution is an inherited problem, but for anyone interested in the present and future environments of Cardiff, the Heliport area is a good place to start investigation – by which I mean walking around the city with open eyes. Considering that recent (that is, before the local elections of May, 1991) council literature announced the intentions of making Cardiff 'the green capital of Europe', such interest should be widespread. Those intentions, shared to a greater or lesser extent by the new Labour dominated council (it depends on who you talk to) rely a good deal on the success of the *Cardiff – Recycling City* scheme, which aims to ensure that by the end of this decade 50 per cent of all domestic waste will be recycled. Bearing in mind that the present figure is under 5 per cent, this is hugely ambitious.

As to the 'green capital' business, the city council has made the first step of a long journey by appointing a co-ordinator for its environmental strategy. This is an enormous task that depends on a flair for good public relations, and what place in the municipal pecking order the city fathers give to the new, genuinely enthusiastic officer. Yet in a European context, considering that the future types of public transport in the city are undecided, and that restrictions on use of the motor car in the centre have hardly been discussed, this is only a very pleasant pipedream. Officials will tell you that Cardiff is one of very few cities in the UK to possess vehicle-exhaust monitoring equipment – on top of the Brains building in St Mary Street. Of course, this is laudable, yet only about as useful as a doctor whose medical bag is empty but for a thermometer. Depressingly, especially for a city with such pretensions, the recently published 'Cardiff Plan' fails almost entirely to tackle this issue.

There is similar doubt about the subject that has dominated Cardiff throughout much of the last decade – the building of a barrage across the mouths of the Taff and Ely rivers, thus creating a lagoon of over 200 acres, and destroying an important site of special scientific interest (SSSI). The fate of the Barrage Bill (the Government has to make a law to break a law, as deliberate SSSI destruction is illegal) remains uncertain, but even to the most casual observer, it is inconceivable that the Cardiff Bay Development Corporation (CBDC), a Government quango with more power, it sometimes appears, than a Venetian oligarchy, and the barrage's other backers, will not strain every muscle to ensure a go-ahead. Their line is simple. The barrage is integral to the whole Bay development, because it will provide Cardiff with an internationally significant waterfront space. A city without water is no city. So dam the rivers.

Opponents have long bludgeoned against the apparent frailty of this argument, but there are simply too many political reputations, local and national, riding on its success. (Note that CBDC was set up by the then Secretary of State for Wales, Nicholas Edwards, now Lord Crickhowell, who also happens to be chairman of the National Rivers Authority, the duty of which is to monitor possible causes of water pollution – and the barrage is an enormous such possible cause.) It is factors such as this that convince many that the barrage was never an environmental matter, but a tightrope that was going to carry its supporters towards the fruits of modest political stardom, or backroom bureaucratic oblivion. Their balancing act continues.

What, however, is emphatically going ahead, is the massive CBDC-inspired redevelopment of much of the south of the city. Those who have not visited Cardiff for some years will be startled by many of the changes, and there are bigger alterations to follow. The Holiday Inn and Wales National Ice Rink buildings were outside the CBDC remit and are now familiar city landmarks. Regarding the latter, I have come to terms with the fact that this arena now sees the only decent sporting activity in the capital. The local soccer team consists of an anonymous bunch of mercenaries, clapped-out cloggers and talent-free work-horses, watched by an increasingly desperate horde of fans who can't even swear in unison, and should be pitied for having nothing better to do on a Saturday afternoon. Meanwhile, it is satisfying to know that the Welsh rugby team has at last achieved a status commensurate with the skills and foresight of its administrators, a body of men who behave with such ritualistic secrecy that they make a Masonic Lodge look like a branch of the Divorced, Separated and Singles Club. But the big yellow hotel appears to me a monument to cultural amnesia and American galumphing bad taste. Strange, but whenever I pass its overpriced bars and lounges, I think of that sickly glop called 'thousand island dressing', with which so many of us seek to ruin a salad.

What the infrequent visitor might not be ready for are the new developments around 'Atlantic Wharf', all in the red and yellow brickwork style of 1970s American marina architecture, which now can be seen at resorts throughout the UK. Of the original structures, the restored Spillers Building stands monumentally, disconcertingly close by, like someone at a boozy wake, refusing to drink. Streets and apartment blocks here have thousand island dressing names: Admirals' Landing, Columbus Walk. Meanwhile, the water in the old Bute East Dock is dead as tarmacadam. Without the vital human ecology that evolved around this once dramatic inner-city work-place, its new role is as a leisure facility for the diners and drinkers in Brains' £3 million 'showpiece' pub, The Wharf. (Note the impressive bronze statue of the dockworker in the foyer. If a labourer came in today dressed like that, he'd be shown the door before he could say 'lasagne and mineral water, please'.) This liquid cul-de-sac also serves, for the drones in South Glamorgan County Council's pagoda-like HQ, as an image for the long-term prospects of a career in paper-shuffling. Whatever, even in the sunniest hours, the fathoms of East Dock are imbued with the urban melancholy of a large car-park, closed on Sunday.

It is this visual, built environment that means most to people when they consider Cardiff, either as home, workplace, or Wales's largest city. Apologists state that the developments are of a scale and ambition appropriate to Europe's newest capital, and remind sceptics of the run-down seedy quality of the streets they have replaced.

This is a good point. Who would bring back the spice markets with their panniers of bismarti and phials of fenugreek? Or The Salutation and The Greyhound, hardly closed to their chalk-faced, acid-bellied habitues before being nudged by the crane's slow sceptre into a fog of brickdust? Or The Half-Moon Club, where the sweat collected like an icy coin in your coccyx? Fewer, probably, than their romanticists would think. It is no good sitting in The New Sea Lock over a maudlin pint of dark, recalling the black jazz-stars of Loudon Square, or the time that Cardiff City went all the way to Tashkent in the European Cup, and took their own tinned spam and tomatoes because the players didn't fancy horse-meat kebabs. It's bite the bullet time, when we have to accept that even Tesco stores come with features like Bavarian bell-towers, and it's the new Bosch and Sony empires just up the road that are calling the shots, not that great man-of-the-people, the Marquis of Bute.

One person who doesn't remember the cider bars and herb shops, is Norma Jarboe, appointed as the manager of Cardiff Marketing, an offshoot of CBDC. A bilingual (Spanish and English) native of New Mexico, Jarboe's rôle is to sell the capital to tourists and investors, to market the Cardiff environment, place to play, a place to work, as a record plugger will cultivate radio producers or disc-jockeys. Understandably, she has nothing to say about the ferrous beaches. That, goes the official line, is an old problem which will be dealt with.

What interests Jarboe are Cardiff's parks and civic buildings, its blueprint of a barrage-created lagoon and the 'climate for leisure' this will nurture, its theatres and cultural life. Well, there's the Opera. But Chapter Arts is a sleazepit now, and there's something about the Sherman Theatre that keeps you forever on the doorstep, never really part of the fun. And isn't St David's Centre only for *côr meibion* evenings and Showaddywaddy revivals? It would be good to think that the politicians who meet in the superb civic district have ideas to match the architecture, and not merely the more commonly associated constricted opinions of an irate car-park attendant, loosed from his hutch. But has anyone told Jarboe of the Cardiff Council commissars' decision not to bid for 'Literature Capital' status under the Arts 2000 initiative, 'because there is only one Welsh writer and that's Dylan Thomas'? And how could Cardiff ever compete, considering its lack of a big city mentality, the absence of sheer size and history, with Dublin and Glasgow for rôles such as 'European City of Culture'? The place doesn't even have an identifiable literary magazine, and apart from the gutsy, defiant but not always literate Red Sharks Press, there's zilch writing activity with more life than East Dock that's not dependent on Arts Council grants.

Nevertheless, Jarboe is a sincere enthusiast for the city that now pays her. She sees it as a product for which she supplies publicity. Cardiff, she claims, echoing many people I have spoken to, is a decent place to live, although it seems sometimes, not a city at all. Climb the Wenallt, Jarboe will urge, shaming perhaps many long-time residents who have never been there, and look down at how the parks run through the capital like thick green arteries. There will come a time, the hype-makers will state, when beach umbrellas will sprout in the reclaimed sands in front of Orchard Ledges, and good Cardiff people who still say Kaardiff will pose with a designer drink in the gardens of the new houses beyond Channel View, brushing away the odd mosquito attracted by the lagoon, and reading the latest *South Wales Echo* editorial about tidal rising. Like it or not, the Cardiff environment is set to change enormously. And some of those changes will determine how visitors and the media portray the rest of Wales to the UK. Yes, it's a decent place, many will say, as long as you don't have to pass the Ferry Road waste tip too often.

This is a humbling and fascinating plateau which makes you re-member why you were born with a nose. In fact, it's the area of Cardiff you see first if arriving from the west via the new Grangetown link. There are three million tonnes of rotting refuse here, all binned over the years by the population of the future green capital of Europe. For a long time it was the CBDC plan to remove the whole lot by lorry and dump it (again) in quarries between neighbouring Welsh boroughs and counties in south-east England. This huge undertaking is now abandoned, raising a major question. For if the Barrage goes ahead, groundwater levels in many areas of the city will rise, creating flood dangers. The prospect of toxic leachate from Ferry Road seeping into higher Cardiff groundwater and thus spreading contamination is one that most exercises the outwardly urbane, not to say self-satisfied, CBDC management reps. Meanwhile, because of lack of space, the Ferry Road tip is now closed. This leaves the Lamby Way site, in the extreme south-east of Cardiff, with a lifetime of five years, as the only repository for the capital's junk. Little wonder that Cardiff desperately requires its Recycling City scheme to work. My advice is, if the city is seriously interested in such matters, invite the Bird Brothers across the Council portals, and pay for some real expertise. But this time, they might expect clean cups.

In a Class of Our Own

The last night of the class was the first I could say I knew my way around the school. This time I wasn't sidetracked down corridors to chemistry labs or flooded toilets. I avoided the basement and the sixth form common room with its fruit machines and exploded armchairs. After nine wet Tuesdays the roped-off piles of building rubble were now familiar landmarks: likewise the rustling drifts of crisp packets trapped against wiremesh. And here was the Youth Wing and a comforting apparition: Spiderman glared from his red and purple mural through a net of his own making. Strange it was always Spiderman the kids painted in these schools. This one's eyes gleamed like nitric acid above the pool cues and table-tennis equipment, his suspended stride seeming to take him over the disc-jockey's plastic hutch. But he stayed there frozen, snared in his own web.

Yoga was warming up; Welsh had reached the evening's first declension. Creative writing, being rather more vague, not to say completely indefinable in its brief, took liberties with the clock. The class had already arrived, and as I ticked the register, the eleven members started opening wine bottles and adding to the school's crisp problem. End of the Christmas term and the whole of the comprehensive was set to become a honeycomb of mild celebration.

'Do you think I've got any then boss?'

'Any what?' My immediate occupation was gouging out the cork from a litre of Rocamar.

'Talent.'

I looked at Cledwyn as hard as I dared. Even his tattoos were spelt wrong. Thirty-five, fortyish, with weasel-red hair in a corrugated perm. Under his shirt the shoulder-muscles were bunches of Fyffes.

'I liked that poem about autumn,' I said. 'Especially where you compare the fallen leaves to cornflakes.'

'Perhaps no-one's ever done that before?'

'Well actually they have. Including George Orwell in some early novel or other. But he didn't mention cornflakes, exactly. It was more some unnamed American breakfast cereal.'

'You mean All Bran?'

'Could well have been. But I think Orwell's purpose was more satirical than, er, literal.'

Cledwyn's narrow eyes became coin-slots. He could tell a phoney a mile away, and a pretentious phoney set the blue vein in his forehead twanging like a guitar string. He drained the last of his Bordeaux Blanc and refilled the styrofoam mug. I turned around to a woman who was pushing a packet of French Niblets across the desk in my direction. As I moved, the broken lid slid to the floor revealing the desk's contents. Crisp packets, coke cans, formica-stiff orange peel. No books of course. In another school a week earlier three boys who passed most of their days playing pool in the Youth Wing had joined a class I was organizing. We had sat under a mural of Spiderman locked in his web and three separate notices forbidding smoking. Around our feet the carpet-tiles were pocked as pumice with cigarette burns, while above us a team of workmen were ripping off the tarred sheeting of the old roof and pouring on the boiling pitch waterproofing of the new. In places this had come through the polystyrene ceiling and congealed in black stalactites. The newcomers had sat down without pens or paper. They had thrown away all their books after their last suspension. They had defeated the system but there was nothing boastful in their voices. Outside a siren had sounded and a thousand children started crossing the asphalt yards, dragging sports bags and anoraks down flaking corridors.

At the time I had experienced a familiar conflict of feelings. The comprehensive method was vital and necessary: moreover, it should apply to everybody. I learned that on the day I passed the eleven plus and my twin sister failed. But comprehensives themselves were hideous places, battery farms that force-fed children a mediocre diet of irrelevant exam-fodder. They were made of plastic and cardboard and the kids rightly kicked them to bits. What was astonishing was the resourcefulness of so many staff and pupils, working in conditions that seemed, to me at least, inevitably alienating. The joylessness of comp-architecture, the impersonal sizes of the schools demanded a protest. Throwing your books away might be as good as any. And perhaps, when they walk around these places, more people than would admit to it have to gulp back some Kingsley Amis-type bile at the brutal functionalness of it all.

But those feelings said more about me than the schools. My horrified fascination with comprehensives seemed to fill the amnesiac's blank I had regarding my own school life. Yet when I dreamed, slept and dreamed, the faces, voices and behaviour of pupils I had not seen for twenty years were intimately recognisable. They were the protagonists in an inescapable haunting. Perhaps, then, you never really leave school, but maintain its small maelstrom of bewilderments and frustrations forever in the subconscious. A hidden pressure. And tonight for some reason, in a different school, my clearest classroom memory was of trying to teach the Spanish Armada to thirty-five third-years in a cubicle designed for twenty. 'Some were blown off course, many sank without trace, while others were wrecked on shores inhabited only by indisciplined Celtic peoples.' Teaching: now there was a real maelstrom for you.

'Not drinking Karen? Brought the car tonight, I suppose.'

'No, it's the pills that stop me. I can't mix pills with wine.'

'Antibiotics? I didn't think you were looking too bright.'

Karen selected a salted biscuit and edged forward. It appeared she took several varieties of tablet, all with unswallowable names.

'I'm a manic-depressive,' she breathed.

'Nonsense. Everyone gets moods.'

'If I mix alcohol with my tablets it's possible I could commit an act that I might regret for the rest of my life.'

I reached for my paper cup with its yellow inch of Liebfraumilch.

'That's terrible.'

'But I'm feeling good tonight. Absolutely bloody brill. And I'm writing at last, I'm really putting stuff down. All that talk in the class the other week, about employment and different jobs, it set me thinking. You see, I used to work in a very strange place.'

Karen eased out another Niblet, her coffee listing dangerously. Some of the others were paying attention now.

'It was a factory back home dealing with what you call sex-aids. I was in packaging, making up the orders.'

'I always had you for a dark horse,' beamed Doreen, our short-story writer. 'I think I'll get my notebook out.'

'There were some really funny experiences with the equipment. Only I don't think I can say their names.'

'Throb,' said Cledwyn emphatically. 'They always use that. It's a fabulous word. Deep Throb. Golden Throb. Throb of Passion. Night Throbber.'

'Well we used to pack up these devices,' whispered Karen. 'But they weren't always reliable. I remember one afternoon we had a new batch of vibrators in, and they all started going off in their boxes. Mr Simpson supervising ran out to the car-park. He thought it was an earthquake.'

Three quarters of an hour's discussion followed on whether class members would wish to write without deadlines and round-the-room criticism. Most, I thought, would not. But John would certainly go on creating his cameos of Rhondda building sites and London high-rise construction. His two-page short stories had a wit and power that we all admired. Perhaps Jean would keep up with her play, Wenfron her poems. And there was Mo, immaculate as ever in Oxfam's finest, blond, beaming and devastatingly camp. I think the class adored him because he proved how powerful a weapon a sense of humour could be. Six years of unemployment had not soured his charm. And perhaps the highlight of the term had been his deadpan accounts of the work offered him by the MSC. Mo had combed his hair, stood up straight, and described waiting in a gents' toilet in Merthyr for four hours, counting how many times the pipes flushed. That was a job. Another job was visiting the bedrooms of hall-of-residence Polytechnic students at 7 a.m. and measuring the air temperature with a thermometer as big as a baseball bat. Back in the present he was busy dispensing the last of the two bottles he had brought in, and toasting the room with a beaker of Tân y Mynydd.

At nine o'clock we returned down the corridors, passing the slippery bogs with their GCSE-really-screws-you-up graffiti. Cledwyn pitched a carafe of Paul Masson on to a loaded skip. He wasn't a bottle-bank man.

'We should do this creative drinking more often. Of course it was originally me who put the pints into poems and pints.'

He paused at the school gate. 'You know I really hated this place. It used to be the old Sec Mod and the bastards crushed you. They caught you by the bollocks and just went on squeezing. They made you think you were dirt. You won't believe this, but I was scared stiff of coming into this class. Enrolment night was the first time I'd ever been back to the school. I even had to take a tablet to walk up that drive. Just thank Christ it's all different now.'

Adult education is a depressing phrase. It makes me think of carburettor overhaul and cheese soufflé, ex-miners blinking at a blackboard haiku. Such classes are the places where great plans founder. New careers should begin there, bestsellers germinate, qualifications multiply. Of course it never works like that. Yet every class that keeps its numbers buoyant above the minimum five is a kind of victory against winter, soap operas, family pressure and forlorn passivity. Perhaps most of all over the wrecked furniture and haemorrhaging damp of modern comprehensives. But really I have little right to think that. Instead of working for change on the inside, I've jumped over the wall, and what I see in the comps are only the symptoms, not the causes, of this blight. And maybe there are schools, who knows, where Spiderman succeeds in more than merely lassoing himself.

Cat's Eyes

Some newspapers refer to it as the 'Crafty Pint Syndrome'. But then they would, wouldn't they? Anything can be described as a syndrome these days. I suppose you'd call it the 'Syndrome Syndrome'. It's something to do with 'leisure time', that scary phenomenon. But there I go again. 'Phenomenon' is another of those words. Thinking about it, life itself could be described as a 'Phenomenon Syndrome'. In some text of the new sciences it probably is. Anyway, this is the scenario.

There is a man (me, of course) a woman and a child. They are on a week's holiday in the country where the woman grew up, but not the man. On the Saturday afternoon of this week, the woman goes off on her own to flick through bookshelves, or racks of clothes, or rooms filled with antique junk, or even for a crafty drink. The child is taken by relatives to the Sports Centre, and can be imagined by at least one of the parents as sliding down a huge plastic funnel into a tropical pool, whilst the lifeguards, slow, tanned, exquisitely bored, pace the waterside, remote in muscled experience from the screams at the wave machine.

And the man? The man is suddenly cut loose, pushed out into the deep end. Alarmed at the prospect of the in-laws' empty front room, the framed photographs, the perfect garden, the inscrutable kitchen, the bedroom where the woman's old school-books lie like invitations to a dance he never heard about, the man starts to float.

Light-headed, as if recovering from an illness, curious at the prospect of no appointments to meet, no meals to make or attend, no people to speak to or be spoken to by, and puzzled by the fuzzy, ridiculous concept of freedom, the man starts to drift down towards the strange town. He goes past entrances to tower-blocks, the stone roof of an ancient, bypass-isolated farm, down through this foreign country into one of its regional capitals.

This is a man who now might have been thrashing a way to an island of plastic palms, or gazing at the spines of paperbacks in an unfamiliar store, a man who is starting to learn the luxury of his own gradual redundancy. So down into the town he goes, past the wire-trailing, plugged-in children, the bus-shelters plastered with posters of the British National Party, a nondescript man in clothes deferential to the weather and the taste of the previous decade.

'What time is it?'

We are cramped together in a tea-brown pew, four foot away from the pool table. Every few seconds one of the large, tattooed pool-players thrusts a bedenimed rump into our faces whilst taking laborious aim over the next shot. We can either stare back impassively at this regular eclipse, or turn away. Perhaps the third choice is to tap one of these gentlemen on the rear and politely request that they all take their fat arses somewhere else.

But arguing the toss with the poolsters is definitely out. All four weigh in on the generous side, whilst one of them, the slowest player, the most painstaking shot-maker, has forearms like building bricks. Not to mention a backside like a Morris 1000. With time to ponder every sag and wrinkle of his blue, elephantine crotch, I consider this marksman to have the lowest centre of gravity of anyone I have ever met. Perhaps it is only this, or some mystical power invested in the heavy Alfa Romeo figurine that he has attached to his belt buckle, that prevents his jeans from slipping below his beer belly down to the tops of his studded biking boots. But he knocks in a colour, sinks the black, and brandishing the cue like an orchestral baton, calls for another can of Bow.

'Five past six,' I reply. The woman who asked the question has been pressed against me for the last fifteen minutes, not because of any feelings of affection she might be harbouring, but because the pub, as they say, is full as an egg. She had come in with a group of people who now occupy the far side of our large table wedged into this annexe of the public bar.

Mustering the courage for an impassive look, I had felt sure about my assessment. Serious pissheads. No question about it. The kind you meet in the shopping precinct on a Saturday afternoon, words slurred by the latest superstrength, bodies engaged in a slow, spastic jive, before they collapse against the redbrick of Tesco and start heckling the trolley-pushing dads.

It's hard to say how far this one has gone. She sips a half and seems to ponder the full depth of my response. Her eyes are bloodshot with large bruises beneath, her hair the last vestiges of a shrivelling perm. Strangely for this darkened bar, populated by men in dangerous heels and tiny vests, by girls in rags of leather and black lace, my companion wears the brilliant, unapologetic uniform of the English working class on its day off.

This is called the shell-suit. Fashioned from material so flimsy and synthetic it makes a crisp-packet feel substantial, the shell-suit is cool, cheap and sexless. Superman could have a hard-on wearing one of these and no-one would notice. It also comes in combinations of any colour as long as they are completely unnatural. Mauve and turquoise, lime-green and puce, tangerine and butterscotch, this all-purpose leisurewear garment, shapeless and crinkly as a cellophane tracksuit, is the new gear for cruising the mall, touring the DIY store or drifting through the theme-park. But not drinking. Someone should tell my cochineal-and-Coke-coloured friend that shell-suits are not serious drinking clothes. If anything she seems to have pushed closer.

'What day is it?'

A violet stratum of cigarette smoke hangs in the air above the beer fug. It's dark, but at least I know, or I think I do, that outside this room the dazzling light of a spring evening is pouring its benedictions through Old Cock Yard and Silver Street, down Black Swan Ginnel and along the cobbles of Hatters Fold. In Albion Street, the fishmongers are tipping their ice into the gutter. It lies like a long shining creature, breathing gently and smoking from the sea. In the terraces behind the Almshouses, the taxis are parked whilst the owners slip home for coffee or television, their children in gorgeous saffrons and scarlets playing touch amongst the Sierras. Down Bonegate Street and Gibbet Street the girls are coming, the early girls in twos and threes, bare-armed in sequinned tops and white cotton trousers, singing and shivering as they head for the centre. At the corner of Trinity Street there is a mild altercation between a young man whose sugar-paper drawings, held down with pebbles, are spread over the pedestrianized sector, and a Securicor van-driver, who thinks the artist is obstructing the road. In red boiler suit, terrier on a leash tied to his ankle, the chalk-handed sketcher stands firm and the driver decides to approach from a different angle. On the flags of the Piece Hall the traders are packing up, and the litter-pickers patrolling with vacs. The rare-stamp dealers are locking their shutters, the buyers of coins and military medals setting alarms, the manager of Masai Mara African Crafts putting straight his facemasks and soapstone talismans. But the punks are still there, in tartan trousers and hair like the shells of horse-chestnuts, lying on the grass in the magnificent light. Tomorrow the stage will be set out for the brass band, and a girl in a blue blazer will arrive clasping a trumpet in a narrow black box. She will sit alone on the stage, without an audience, and clip a clothes-peg to some sheet music. Pensioners and children will occupy the benches, and petrol-coloured pigeons leave their roosts among the colonnades for the gullies between cobbles. On the steps of the Halifax Building Society a stranger will pause, sit down, and write a few words onto a scrap of paper. And even in that quiet, sparsely-populated evening, people will glance at him, and turn away. No-one writes in public. And the stranger will look up at this temple, at the tall wrought-iron sculpture on its forecourt rusting into a pool of rainwater, the glass of the walls returning his scrutiny with the anonymous stare of sunglasses. The revolving doors will spin but no-one enter, no-one leave, and the computers, with their gold screens and totalitarian memories remain untouched, like unvisited shrines.

'Saturday,' I say, into the inch high foam of a pint of Tetley's, winking at me like tiny eyes. 'All day.' The girl is probably only twenty, but looks older. Either it's the drink that has placed the rosettes in each cheek, or she's been crying. In the pub light it is now difficult to tell. Everything is reduced after a while here to districts of grey, colours, like faces, running into one another. She reminds me of a photograph I saw today in the industrial museum.

I had stood beside a moquette loom on a factory floor filled with sunlight and swirling dust. The threads were pulled tight, and against the window, shone like a rainbow with the colours shuffled. On the wall the picture showed a long chamber, filled with women. There must have been hundreds in the background, pale-faced and indistinct in the gloom like flowers in an evening garden.

They were toffee wrappers. They spent all day putting the wax-paper twists around thousands of toffees, after the men of the factory had cut the sweets from huge table-tops of caramel.

121

Women were given this work because their fingers were thought to be nimbler. In the foreground of the picture was one girl, dark-lipped, a ribbon in her hair, the age of the singers in Bonegate Street on their way to an evening of bacardis and lasers. And her look was as frank as if you were buying a pound of Mackintosh's from her today at Woolworth's. But this is the toffee-wrapper's day off, and she seems determined to drink her way out of any distress she has brought with her to this public room.

England, I suppose, has always been a mystery to me. That's why I'm here at the 'Portman and Pickles', which seemed a few minutes ago as good a place as any to begin investigations. The trouble is, I'm too late. I should have come sooner when there were answers to be had. But England was always a foreign country, a little too far down the A38 for a comfortable day out. Now one week a year isn't enough. I can't catch up. The truth is, before I was twenty, the only time I visited England I was aged ten, and the invasion reached as far as Bristol Zoo.

There were a pair of white tigers there, considered a great rarity and a wonderful advertisement for the city. I looked at the tigers as they paced the concrete floor of a cage the size of a double garage. They were not white but pale lemon, and their stripes might have been the faint shadows of the cage-bars. It was impossible to catch their eyes as they determinedly pretended we weren't there. Perhaps for the tigers we truly didn't exist, but remember wishing that they would look up and recognise that I, of all the people who would stand around the cage that day, bore them no malice. That I understood. The animals patrolled a circuit over the same straw where they had tried to bury their shit. Soon after this we had left, and I can recall having a slight car accident, the vehicle behind running into us as we slowed down at a junction.

As a race, the English are a dangerous hybrid. They are the human equivalent of Japanese knotweed, a plant discovered in the unlikeliest settings. Removing it is virtually impossible, due to the tenacity of its root system, the thickness of its skin. But this is its home territory, a few hours drive from where I have spent my life.

There's no excuse, I should have come earlier and more frequently. It feels now as if I'm dangerously late for something. This afternoon I walked up a flight of worn mill steps to the top of town.

There's a car-park there, for the sole use, the notices say, of the employees of a particular bank. It was immaculately empty, a dark tarn of asphalt behind immobile traffic barriers. From there the town is on show like some matchstick model in a museum case, surprising spires in every direction, an ornate council chamber, mill buildings turned into honeycombs of offices and workshops, and beyond them all, the olive slopes of the high ground, curiously voluptuous in the afternoon light. On one of the steeper hills was a geometrical stripe, like a razor mark through stubble. That was the ski-slope, crowded with people wearing bright ski-clothes, skidding and tumbling down the taut ropework of the piste.

From that summit, you could see where the weather would change, even predict when the bruise would appear on the horizon. Already there was a sinew in the wind, and I came down to street-level, to the Saturday evening festival and the sand-blasted frontage of the 'Portman and Pickles', called, presumably, after local radio and theatre personalities. So I had taken my place under the video screen, locked by an industrial bolt to the ceiling, settling down on the exploded red plastic of the bench, out of which protruded an intestinal foam, and found all faces turned in my direction.

'I reckon there's billions by now,' muttered someone on my left, one of the few in the bar uninterested in what was happening above my head. 'If you added them all up, there definitely ought to be billions.'

He was an old man with a deerstalker, a trembling cigar, and a pint that looked too full for him. His face had a yellow tinge, and the skin around his eyes was delicate as tissue paper, dark with lines.

'Think about it. France, Australia, the Pan American Highway, the M62, Spaghetti Junction. They've all got them, or a lot of them have got them. And if they haven't got them yet they're going to get them. All of them.'

It was not obvious that he was talking to me.

'Got what?'

He tested the bitter like a dubious medicine.

'Reflecting road studs. Billions of them. Think about it.'

Above my head something was coming to a conclusion. I could tell by the furrowed brows and communal leer of the group of boys opposite, all with their eyes ceiling-wards, all with vertical hair, shorn with ski-slopes. Already he was speaking again.

'Lived round here he did, you know. Just up the road. Patented the stud and made his fortune. Used to come in here when it was a pub, he still had time for a jar. Think about it. All those cat's eyes winking all over the world. And him gone cold a while since.'

A few minutes later the deerstalker was gone and the glass empty except for a halo of foam. And now the bar is even more crowded and the pool players lining coins up on the side of the table. The toffee-wrapper continues to glare, with some male-volence, at the yellow effervescence in her lager. Fidgeting, she is turning towards me again, wrestling with the mysterious compulsion to make words. Watching the bubbles rise and disappear in her drink, I know exactly what she is going to say.

Reading the Zones

1. Eastern

The students have gone to lunch, their placards left on the lawns. 'No War in the Gulf', 'Give Peace a Chance', and the ambiguous 'Between Iraq and a Hard Place' are daubed in mapleleaf-crimson amongst the flowerbeds. My hosts are impressed. They have just spent the last two hours driving me from Boston to Keene in New Hampshire, and used most of the time in the car to describe the apathy, the conservative, head-down, work-for-a-career attitude of many American students. To find political sentiment suddenly penetrating the torpor is a pleasant surprise.

In Lecture Room Two the sentiment is developed to such an extent that in ninety minutes I manage to read only seven poems. The rest of the session is taken up with answering the questions of two hundred young men and women scattered around a hall that feels the size of a Roman amphitheatre. The ranks of seats are so steep that I get a stiff neck looking at the students farthest away. There is no p.a. or glass of water, but a dutiful bout of clapping after each piece of verse. This is disconcerting. Applause at a poetry reading is like encountering your old English teacher in the pub toilet. The questioning grows louder and more confident.

'Isn't Wales like New Hampshire? I mean, all the rich people in Boston come here and buy the farms.'

'Aren't there still Druids in Wales? I read they all get together at Christmas and speak in tongues.'

'I'm from the Basque Country and I support the terrorist action there. Aren't people like you who use the English language while claiming to be Welsh just a part of the problem?'

From the auditorium I take a small cheque, an escort to the basketball court, and an icy nettlerash of perspiration in the small of my back. 'Christ, they should draft those kids', says the genial lecturer who arranged the visit. He is blond, fit, popular and looks about eighteen. He has also bought a Keene State sweatshirt for my daughter, and thus is now elevated to her pantheon of personal heroes, somewhere between Madonna and Morticia Addams. 'The logic bomb – it's our new secret weapon. We could vaporize Baghdad.'

And logic has it that after every poetry reading at Keene, the poets get a free hour in one of the best equipped gymnasiums in the state. So we play catch, practice a little clumsy, half-hearted soccer and are slowly drawn next-door to watch the girls' volley-ball squad going through a routine on a training court that would be wasted on most international teams. Sport, of course, is more important than religion here. And every game has its Mount Olympus of gods and super-heroes. Each night, the TV overdoses on huge quantities of ice hockey, football and basketball, sports that might once have had some connection with ordinary people, but which are now neurotically-choreographed rituals, domi-nated by the grotesque, the gargantuan and the deformed. The gladiators of these charades are permanently grossed-out on a diet of steroids, painkillers and media hype. (Perhaps we should exclude Michael Jordan of the Chicago Bulls, and Larry Bird of the Boston Celtics from this. They actually look, and play, like athletes.)

Nevertheless, the freaks of football and basketball are household names to millions of TV sickos. And as the demand for success becomes ever more hysterical, so the pressure mounts to recruit bigger, better players. Genetic engineering could be one answer. After all, here in New England, scientists are experimenting with animals that might once have been hogs. Today they are immobile, enormous pork machines, fed on garbage and human shit. Bowing to the pressure, the top US basketball teams are now scouring Africa for the tallest men in the world. One, a seven foot six inch wretch from The Gambia has recently been shipped over by a major club. There's no more meat on him than a New York sparrow, and in interview he stoops apologetically, the expensive suit hanging like a tent around his skeletal chest. The star grunts and smiles and looks as forlorn as the dodo in Manhattan's Museum of Natural History.

Out of the gym, we drive to Mount Misery, all of 258 feet above sea-level in the Massachusetts woods, and start to climb. The idea had been to visit Walden Pond, but the traffic that had been visible around its minor roads had deterred us. Walden, like much of rural America, is a victim of leisure. Jet-skiers and power-boat racers erode its banks and foul its waters. Now a saviour has appeared who wants to put everything back as it was. To pay for it, he is asking that one small, exclusive, tasteful, authentic log-cabin time-share be allowed on its banks. Thoreau himself would not have objected. In fact, he would have been first to put his name down. The planning jury is still out.

Below Mount Misery is a lake larger than Walden. Yet no-one knows what it is called. Its waters are as dark as tea and filled with the leaves of sumacs and oaks. Around its shore grows a plant with an Indian name and tiny red berries that we are instructed to eat. They taste of pepper and warm cloves. Looking into the pool, I remember the Boston Aquarium we had visited yesterday. Everywhere in the city people had asked us to vote for various candidates in the state elections. The whole of America was voting, for Governors, Senators, Attorney Generals, various bills, referenda and environmental imperatives. We escaped them, and the freezing Boston wind, by entering the Mount Misery-like gloom of the Aquarium.

That's where we met the sandtiger. This is a fairly modest member of the shark family, often found in the waters off New England. Through the glass we were able to look into its anthracite eyes. It would be interesting to learn how genetic engineers might think they could improve sharks. Bigger steaks, smoother skin, easier to catch, perhaps. But what would they make of the shark's remote, Jurassic soul? I stood in front of the sandtiger shark and fingered the damp literature of the wrestling Republicans and Democrats that filled my pockets. The female sandtiger shark apparently, has a double uterus. When she becomes pregnant, two baby sharks begin to develop, one in each uterus. But one always grows faster. One always grows bigger, and is more essentially, genetically, spiritually a sandtiger shark, than the other embryo. So the stronger eats the weaker. It breaks into the other uterus and devours its womb-mate. Like a real sandtiger shark should. And then it is born.

2. Central

Doug, the student who picked me up from the airport at Indianapolis, is apologetic.

'We should have snow by now,' he says. 'It should be colder. All this,' he gestures over the steering wheel, 'well, it's kinda weird.'

We're entering Crawfordsville, home of about twelve thousand Hoosiers. Indiana number plates all boast of 'Hoosier hospitality', and certainly the weather they provide is welcoming. Around the campus of Wabash College and the town's quiet avenues, people walk in shirtsleeves and tee-shirts. Above them stand the naked trees, at their feet lie the great crimson drifts of oak and maple leaves. A wind as warm as diesel exhaust caresses the parking-lot of the General Lou Wallace Motel, where I'm booked for two nights.

Doug disappears and I am left in a big, twilit room, furnished with twin double-beds and a monumental television set. There's no point in unpacking, I reason with myself. My clothes are already impossibly creased, and even if I succeed in excavating them from the rucksack, I will never get them back in. Switching on the cable channel, I discover the General Lou Wallace Restaurant has a corned-beef special all day for four dollars. This slightly undercuts the Noble Roman Pizzeria down the street, which, however, carries Doug's enthusiastic endorsement. On a local news channel a young woman is discussing the widely forecast Mid-West earthquake. Apparently the most favoured location for this looming catastrophe is central Indiana.

For a twenty-year old, Doug had been depressingly well-travelled and articulate. Everything I knew about Crawfordsville I owed to him. Like the fact that in American history, there are two celebrated Crawfordsvillians. First of these by a mile is the already familiar General Lou Wallace, soldier of the Civil War, and author of 'Ben Hur'. Crawfordsville is grateful to the General for putting it on the map. So much so that there is a Ben Hur Museum and an annual Ben Hur 'Circus Maximus', which, according to Doug, I had just missed. There is also the pink neon hoarding out in the lot, now eternalizing the military hero and literary legend in the warm dusk, as he advertizes cocktails and corned-beef.

There is, however, no tribute to Crawfordsville's other famous son, Ezra Loomis Pound. About 1908, Pound, still in his early twenties had arrived from Kellog, Idaho, and taken a post as lecturer at Wabash College. Pound, by this time, was not only a poet, he looked like one, apparently sporting a golden earring, seductive curls, and a dandy's taste in clothes and liquor. A great success with the students, Pound had frequented the taverns of Crawfordsville, finding after classes, that the town offered few other attractions. There is, of course, one apocryphal story, of a bar-room encounter between the bored Wabash tutor and the, by then, rather senior General Wallace. What the writers made of each other's work is not recorded.

A tavern, however, proved Pound's downfall at Wabash. Doug had explained this most sensitive part of the story with touching apologies. Apparently at the time, Wabash had been an all male college. 'And you're never gonna believe this,' Doug had laughed as he drove me in the borrowed Buick through the beanfields of Montgomery County. Ahead of us the road was as straight as a runway. 'It still is.' I remember his eyes turned away from the highway, looking expectantly for my reaction. Signs for Peru, Lebanon, Smartboro flashed by. 'Apart from the military academies, we're the last in the whole country. Like we're unique.'

Pound, so the legend goes, had been drinking in town. During the evening he had met a woman from a burlesque show who was stranded in Crawfordsville. Her companions had taken the last train, and here she was, without money or friends or a bed for the night.

The next morning the poet had gone to the classroom as usual at 9 a.m. leaving the dancer still asleep in his rooms. Soon after, the chamber-maid entered, and was surprised to find this guest. The news was relayed to the Dean, with what still seems like extraordinary haste, and at 10 a.m. Pound was summoned to his office. And sacked.

Eighty years later, there is no motel or hoarding or plaque that might tell the visitor that Crawfordsville was once home to Ezra Pound. Even the College remains embarrassed by the incident, although for the whole of the US literary establishment, the poet is a difficult case.

But there is no trace of censoriousness this evening as the

English Department welcomes me with food, drink, books and a small audience. I read for an hour and am then swamped with apologies for the fact that only twenty people have turned up. 'But even Ezra Pound wouldn't have got more,' is the general consensus. Apparently 'The Simpsons' is on television tonight, a thirty minute period when the streets clear, and America's newest anti-hero, the terrifying Bart, acned, wise-cracking, hair like a potato-crisp, occupies the prime-time. According to the professors, Bart Simpson is a fount of pre-pubescent world-weariness. His cynicism is breathtaking, his social observation hot as lime pickle, his contempt for his parents so absolute that it could possibly corrode the whole tradition of American family life. 'We should send him to Iraq,' claims one of the lecturers, pouring apple juice from an enormous plastic pitcher. Wabash is an alcohol- as well as a woman-free zone. 'But the UN would probably object.'

Back at the Lou Wallace I can find no trace of Bart Simpson on any of the seventeen channels that are beamed into Crawfordsville. But there is tomorrow's special at the Noble Roman and a man who is asking if Saddam Hussein is worse than Hitler, how come we escorted him all around the Colorado nerve-gas bases when he was a colonel in the Iraqi army. According to Wabash, all the burlesque shows now give Crawfordsville a miss, so I turn to a book I have been given. This is the long lost novel 'Fall Quarter' by the long lost Weldon Kees, a poet, painter and jazz musician, who is supposed to have walked off San Fransisco's Golden Gate Bridge in 1955. 'It's hot from the Storyline Press this week', said someone from the faculty. 'You'll be the first ever person from the UK to read it.' The dustjacket states that Kees's fate 'remains conjectural', as he had spoken of changing his identity in Latin America. Kees's hero is a twenty-five year old tutor, taking up his first job at a mid-West college. As the young man arrives in town, what he notices first is the weather. The wind is a warm, acrid exhaust blowing towards him down the street. A pink neon hoarding glows in the dusk.

3. Mountain

Waking in the dark, I feel cold. I also feel slightly breathless, as if I had been walking uphill, or cycling, or anything apart from dreaming about something I have already forgotten. Stretching, I discover how large the bed is, a cool acre in which I am pinioned. It is as if a nearby smoker had exhaled a scentless draught into my face. Then I remember. I am in Santa Fe, which is two miles above sea-level. Or more accurately, I am in a house above a canyon near the village of Tesuque, on the road to Taos.

Outside there's snow on the ground, and a few red apples on the trees, good for nothing now but horse-mash. The dark tarn of rainwater in the swimming-pool canvas is frozen hard. In my porch there's a collection of coloured minerals and pine cones. The silver carapace of a beetle shines in a corner like a roll of dimes. There's mist around the ponderosa pines below me in the canyon, and trails of smoke from nearby homes. But the day is warm. I open the garden-gate and walk in shirtsleeves into the New Mexico State Forest, one and a half million acres, give or take a mountain range, of uninhabited wilderness.

Last night the coyotes had been loud and close, and climbing onto the mesa, I discover their perfect tracks in the silt of a dry arroyo. There are blue jays in the cactus, and mule deer scittering through the juniper. That bed was an experience. That was a five star bed, a film-star bed. In fact, one of the last people to sleep in it had been Robert Redford, who had stayed in Tesuque while making a movie about New Mexico. One day, the legend goes, he had climbed up here on to the mesa for a twenty minute jog. Four and a half hours later he had reappeared below, whey-faced and exhausted.

It's easy to get lost up here. The pinon pine and juniper only grow to ten feet in height, but every trail through the trees looks the same, every arroyo, every cactus exactly like the one you passed five minutes ago. Very carefully, very slowly, I walk half a mile into the forest, and sit under a dead trunk on a cold outcrop of quartz, polished like a kidney. There are nameless birds here, and yellow flowers on the cactus. Grey ribbons of paper-dry snow lie in the shadows of rocks. I turn to my notebook. The last entry reads: 'Nov. 19, 4 p.m. Sign in airport lounge. It reads: *"Welcome to Denver, the Mile-High City. If you appear forty or younger you will be asked for identification for service of alcoholic beverages".'* And a mile high is as high as you're gonna get.

I think of the schoolgirls at home, gaudy as jays, queueing at The Pier for bacardis, and the Denver barmen in their striped aprons, enormous badges that warn 'We Always ID' on their lapels. And even more clearly see the man who had sat across the aisle from me on the flight into Albuquerque last night. They had had to delay the aeroplane for him, and he arrived drenched in sweat, fanning himself with a magazine. 'Hot mama tonight!' he had gasped, as the stewardesses had begun their ministrations. 'Jeez,' he laughed, looking at me for support. 'This is an awesome planet. Eight miles into the stratosphere and they're giving us peanuts.'

Walking very carefully I find my way back across the mesa, and at dusk hear the coyotes again as I head for town. Once more they are in good voice, maintaining an eerie wailing in the pinon. Perhaps they have seen Redford's film. In Santa Fe all around the Plaza, the Indians are packing up after a day hawking jewellery and beautiful rugs, whilst the Californicators, behind their shades and suntans, are looking in the windows of real estate agents.

New Mexico is changing, but older ways of life survive. In the mountains there has been a cash economy only since the last war. Before that, most services were done in kind. Out of town, much of the best land is owned by the tribes, Hopi, Zuni, Navajo, Apache, and those with names you never hear in Westerns. They also own the water. What the Indians don't like, apart from each other, are tourists. They're not particularly fond, either, of the old Spanish-speaking populations of the state. But it's here, and in the far north-west, that aboriginal peoples maintain their strongest presence in the whole of the country. In Indiana, there were a few remnants of the Potawatomees; even in suburban Boston and long-settled New England, Indian languages and traditions survive. But here, in their red adobe villages, protected really by the general lack of settlers, the last of the first peoples are able to hang on. Meanwhile, an ominous hour has arrived. Walking across the street to the bookstore, it strikes me that I might be about to perform one of the most ludicrous acts of my life. And in public, too. For a moment, zone-weary, culturally-confused, sunburnt and cactus-stabbed, I have mislaid my ID.

4. Pacific

November 22 is Thanksgiving. It was also the date, twenty-seven years ago, on which John Kennedy was assassinated by, most people here now seem to believe, a team of gunmen who have never been brought to trial. So where were you on that famous day? asks a succession of TV programmes and newspaper articles. The stars describe in whose pool, on which filmset, they were building their careers, when the news came through. Personally, I was aged eleven, and taking the back off a radio in my bedroom, examining its delicate glowing organs and racing through a blur of short wave static when I tuned into the Home Service and heard the flash. So where were we when they sawed off the top of Kennedy's head and stole his brain? Where was Richard Nixon and the men in suits with voices like iguanas'? Some questions don't get answered.

And they don't get asked today in Port Angeles, a small town that sits quietly and exhales smoke under the shadow of the forests of the Olympic peninsula. Across the straits the grey smudge of land is Canada. Somewhere out there, in the complications of fjord and inlet, island and promontory, the piebald killer whales get a day off from the tourists, and dolphins cruise the sea's empty mall. I sit with an egg-nog as the Cowboys and the Redskins pause for another commercial, and the rain comes down in long clear fusillades, like the needles of the ponderosa pine. Mist covers Mount Olympus as densely as it hides the Muncheese pizzeria and the Toyota dealership at the end of the road.

'So how do you feel about the fuss back home?' my host enquires.

'What fuss?'

'The fuss now she's gone.'

'Who's gone?'

'Your Maggie, that's who's gone. She resigned this morning.'

I suppose in years to come, people will ask, where were you when you heard Mrs Thatcher had been assassinated? I was in a suburban lounge with six inches of egg-nog, and an icy relay of martinis starting to circulate. I was sitting on a sofa making occasional remarks to a plastic flower on the sideboard. Ingenious toy, the sunflower bowed and smiled towards you, like a deaf aunt, whenever a noise was made in its direction. That's where I was, I will say.

And that's my Thanksgiving over. For the rest of the day I experience a weird jetlag, a disassociation, a withdrawal period. The Thanksgiving bird sizzles on the table, but it's cold turkey for all Thatcher junkies around the world. The sweet potatoes, the dark meat, the white meat, the cauldron of cranberries perform vanishing acts, but I feel that Mount St. Helens, which I will pass tomorrow on the road to Portland, has erupted again. The air is filled with a black fall-out of tribute, astonishment, recrimination. British politicians with incredible accents bubble thick as lava on at least three of the twenty-seven channels. Mrs Thatcher comes out of a conference, she is standing in the Commons, and there is Mr Kinnock, like Bart Simpson with a hideous Welsh gloat, and here she is again, departing in a limousine almost half the size of the baby-blue Lincoln, boasting more chrome than a fire-engine, that my host uses for a run-around.

Now it's pass-the-parcel with the whiskey-sours, but the DTs (Departure of Thatcher) have got me good. We're going to have to put the country in the Betty Ford Clinic. So where were you when.... I was in my room with the venetian blinds pulled tight. The radio with its case unscrewed looked like one of those towns in the flat, square states. Iowa, Missouri. Towns like the backs of radios, all bunches of wires and winking buttons, and surrounding them the fields, smooth and neat like ironed laundry. You look at them for hours before you finally pull the vizor down on the aeroplane window and call for a long one.

'You say that freckled dude with the smirk is Welsh? And they're gonna make him *President*?'

The Cowboys launch another surge, and I'm still blurred, still ragged at the edges the next day when we motor through Washington State's monsoons towards Portland. The heaviest rain in 110 years and the Cadillac sticks to a sullen 50 as it goes in and out of the car-wash. We play driving music, bad weather music, music to relax by, nodding to the rhythm like three conversational sunflowers. On the dashboard is a rank of switches labelled 'climate control'. Whatever the hurricane does outside, all we hear is the sibilance of the air-conditioning, as the temperature within the Cadillac stays a constant 65°F and the Macks go past with their horizontal segments of Oregon forest. The fields are flooded, the interstate a rink. Farms we pass have enormous satellite dishes close to the house to pick up as much TV as possible. Each one's a flat, fenced Goonhilly. In Brownsville someone boasted to me that they had counted six hundred and twenty-five different channels, including Japanese economics and Filipino porn. Man, you wouldn't believe some of the things you can get these days on the tube.

Portland looks deserted, but Powell's Bookstore swarms with customers. It is by far the largest bookshop I have ever seen, bigger it seems than New York's Strand. An adjoining warehouse has been turned into the store's own two level carpark, whilst inside the shop is a teeming café where browsers can read unhindered for hours, over coffee and desserts, and never feel pressurized into actually purchasing what they study. The whole town's here, in silent contemplation of the miles of shelves, motionless with a blueberry muffin over computer science and lit. crit. I try to imagine the trillions of words, like atoms of a disintegrated star. For anyone who has ever published a line, this is the place to have your ego crushed, your reputation left stained and wrinkled at the back of the filing cabinet. But there's no room between the steaming gaberdine and dripping cagoules, no space for a sodden claustrophobic. I break out to the dark street and see that my name, with the accompanying phrase 'Welsh poet tonight' is glowing in weird blue neon above the entrance.

Cyd's Cocktails is the nearest refuge, a twilight cellar with fifteen video screens showing close-ups of bodybuilders oiling themselves and bikers squeezing into leather. The place feels like a gymnasium with mirrored walls. At every corner and table sits a solitary man with a small drink, tapping a cigarette.

'I really thought she'd duke it out,' someone says in the darkness, but I am transfixed by the heavy goblet the barman pushes in front of me, three fingers of sourmash steaming on the rocks. And five minutes later find myself standing behind the p.a. at Powell's, adding to the word flood. A hundred faces, ninety per cent with spectacles, peer up at me over waxed paper coffee cones and cinnamon bagels. The till rings like a non-stop telephone, the waitresses circulate with trash-baskets, and forty minutes later I am asking for questions. The owl-eyed congregation frowns, thinks, and returns to the interrupted texts of Sunday night in Portland. I feel guilty for stealing their time. But as I contemplate returning to Cyd's subterranean bourbon factory, a woman approaches. She takes off her glasses and rubs them with the cuff of her raincoat.

'You are from Wales?' she asks, so softly that I have to apologise twice.

'If so, can you tell me whether there are any druids still living in your neighbourhood?'

'Of course,' I say, clearing up my papers. 'Lots of them. And what's good is they've even started their own TV channel.'

5. Eastern

We're on Madison, somewhere in the high 70s, in a gallery. This, my host insists, is going to be exclusive. Although there are already three hundred people in the rows of seats, and crowds more in knots around the exhibits, these invitations are gold-dust. So I sit and wait, relaxed, redundant, at the end of everything. Tonight, let somebody else do the talking. Antique, fierce radiators roast the air, but in a city that throws away more trash than most countries, there's not a paper cup to be had, not a plastic mug of diet seltzer or caffeine-free mineral enhanced fruit substitute to drain and crush and add to the barge-loads of reeking garbage that pass the Statue of Liberty every day on their journeys to the landfills at Cold Kills.

So we wait and the crowd thickens and the air dries and then the Publisher comes on. He's been publishing this magazine for twenty-five years, and boy, oh boy has it been.... He starts to list some of the famous names that have graced its pages. I don't recognise any of them, but seven years ago I once received a rejection slip from this prestigious journal. Twenty-five years and twenty-five minutes later we are at the end of the alphabet, and the Publisher introduces the Editor who will introduce the four

Poets we have reading this evening. I look at her earrings. They are spring waterfalls through New Hampshire snow. I look at the buckle on her designer jeans. It is one of the enormous rhomboids of ice that are naturally shovelled into your glass in even the meanest New York bar. But most of all I look at her paper cup, from which she sips when she needs to clear her throat. The Editor clears her throat a good deal tonight, as if she was expelling particles of a particularly unwholesome poem that had lodged somewhere in her digestive system. The shadow in the paper cup grows smaller, her buckle returns the flashes of the cameras, her eyes maintain the steady green stare of a deep-freeze.

The first poet has a stammer. His hair is barbered so savagely you can see the veins in his head bulging with the effort of performing in public. My host leans over and tells me that this was one of the first campaigners against a nuclear base near New London. He actually got on to one of the submarines and pad-locked himself to a rail. The poet drops his papers, he can't find the piece he wants to read, he starts something, wrinkles his nose, abandons it. On the table in front of him he has placed a very tall glass of some colourless liquid. Between poems, during poems, and as an alternative, it seems, to any form of banter with the audience, the reader frequently grabs for the grog and performs a curious gargling ritual. My host leans closer. He explains that the reader's Collected Poems are appearing next year, he's coming to the UK on a reading tour, he's.... The applause is ecstatic. It's immense, incredible. A man to my left, a man with a large plastic beaker of what looks very much like red wine shouts 'More!' I look at his lips, his broad, grey American lips. I watch them as without effort, without embarrassment, they form that one astonishing word.

I look at this man with interest. How, I ask myself, how can I hate, how can I so profoundly detest someone to whom I have never even been introduced? How can I do that? The man is still clapping when the next reader walks on.

This is a poet who has given up poetry. He's become an independent film studio scriptwriter. This poet writes stories about a man called Buddy Knox. The Buddy Knox stories, are, apparently, pretty well known on the high 70s on Madison. Buddy Knox used to be a poet before he started writing stories. Buddy Knox used to do readings at galleries on Madison Avenue. Buddy Knox is an independent film studio scriptwriter at the end of his rope. He has coke problems, wife problems, girlfriend problems, children problems, alimony problems. He can't write anymore. He can't get an erection. His best friend has AIDS. His bosses are about to cut him out of everything. But Buddy Knox has one last idea, one last dream. He has a script about a writer. The writer used to be a poet but now he's an independent film studio scriptwriter at the end of his rope. His name is Art Seicko. Art Seicko has drink problems, wife problems, girlfriend problems, children problems. He can't write anymore, his best friend has cancer, he can't get an erection. His bosses are about to give him the bullet. But Art Seicko has one last idea that just might, just could possibly work.

Buddy Knox is describing his day in a story from the next collection of Buddy Knox stories. He is driving down a street in L.A. Tomorrow the repo man comes to take back the car. In a brown bag between Buddy's thighs is a bottle of Stoly he has just retrieved from the fridge. It's so cold it's still steaming, he can feel it burning through the thin linen of his slacks. Meanwhile, Buddy is pondering the fact, the unignorable, indisputable fact, that everyone in this world, everybody on this pitiful planet has either, Buddy says to himself, has either got a cock or a cunt. You know, like everybody, says Buddy. And that's everybody. There is no exception. Buddy goes on to describe in detail some of the organs he can imagine nestling in the crotches of the Olds and Honda drivers that pass him on the interstate. San Diego slips by and he's still giving us the close-ups. Because this is Buddy's Damascus Highway. This is illumination. This is awesome and then some. And as Act Two of the symphony of applause starts its thunder, my host leans over.

'This guy is one cool operator. People love the bastard. They understand his problems, you know the divorce, the booze. We can all relate to that. They tell me he's doing a UK tour next year, he's....'

As the clapping dies and the interval begins, the man sitting directly ahead of me turns round. 'Excuse me,' he says, 'but I could hear you talking before the start. You're Welsh aren't you, you're bloody Welsh.'

He squeezes out of his row and squats down in the aisle. 'It's amazing, I've been here five years and you're the first Welsh person I've met in all that time. Scots, Irish, they're all over the place, but the Welsh, we must just blend in. We disappear. Look, we've got to meet up at the end of this and have a drink. A friend gave me the invitation, but I don't know if I can stand any more of it. All poets are creeps as far as I'm concerned. Like seriously weird as we don't say in Swansea.'

The Welshman stands up, and wipes sweat from the corners of both eyes. As I shift in my seat he turns and looks harder at me. 'You know it's great to meet you. And I can't wait to know what you're doing over here.'